Praise for *The Hidden Symmetry of Your Birth Date*

*"The wisdom Jean Haner presents in **The Hidden Symmetry of Your Birth Date** has been valuable in my own life over the years. I highly recommend it as a way to love and accept yourself, as well as the way your life is unfolding. I'm delighted to contribute the affirmations in this book to support your journey!"*

— **Louise L. Hay**, the *New York Times* best-selling author of *You Can Heal Your Life*

*"**The Hidden Symmetry of Your Birth Date** will help you to know yourself, accept yourself, and be true to who you really are. Jean Haner presents an ancient wisdom for living an authentic life. Her work is a gift to the world."*

— **Robert Holden, Ph.D.**, author of *Shift Happens!* and *Loveability*

*"Jean Haner's book **The Hidden Symmetry of Your Birth Date** will take you into the deepest recesses of your being, where you can begin to answer those questions such as 'Who am I?' and 'Why am I here?' With grace and wisdom born of an innate understanding of the human spirit, Jean will gently guide you down the path to profound self-understanding in this heartfelt book. Highly recommended!"*

— **Denise Linn**, author of *Soul Coaching* and *Sacred Space*

*"In **The Hidden Symmetry of Your Birth Date**, Jean Haner draws on a little-known but powerful ancient knowledge to provide readers with invaluable clues to an authentic, rich, and meaningful life. Combined with the timeless insights of Louise Hay's affirmations, the book will be an inspiring and unique addition to any seeker's library."*

— **Lorie Eve Dechar**, author of *Five Spirits*

THE HIDDEN SYMMETRY OF YOUR BIRTH DATE

How Your Birth Date Reveals
the Plan for Your Life

JEAN HANER

HAY HOUSE

Carlsbad, California • New York City • London • Sydney
Johannesburg • Vancouver • Hong Kong • New Delhi

First published and distributed in the United Kingdom by:
Hay House UK Ltd, Astley House, 33 Notting Hill Gate, London W11 3JQ
Tel: +44 (0)20 3675 2450; Fax: +44 (0)20 3675 2451
www.hayhouse.co.uk

Published and distributed in the United States of America by:
Hay House Inc., PO Box 5100, Carlsbad, CA 92018-5100
Tel: (1) 760 431 7695 or (800) 654 5126
Fax: (1) 760 431 6948 or (800) 650 5115
www.hayhouse.com

Published and distributed in Australia by:
Hay House Australia Ltd, 18/36 Ralph St, Alexandria NSW 2015
Tel: (61) 2 9669 4299; Fax: (61) 2 9669 4144
www.hayhouse.com.au

Published and distributed in the Republic of South Africa by:
Hay House SA (Pty) Ltd, PO Box 990, Witkoppen 2068
Tel/Fax: (27) 11 467 8904
www.hayhouse.co.za

Published and distributed in India by:
Hay House Publishers India, Muskaan Complex, Plot No.3, B-2,
Vasant Kunj, New Delhi 110 070
Tel: (91) 11 4176 1620; Fax: (91) 11 4176 1630
www.hayhouse.co.in

Distributed in Canada by:
Raincoast, 9050 Shaughnessy St, Vancouver BC V6P 6E5
Tel: (1) 604 323 7100; Fax: (1) 604 323 2600

Copyright © 2013 by Jean Haner

Cover design: Rhonda Dicksion • *Interior design:* Nick C. Welch

The moral rights of the author have been asserted.

The information given in this book should not be treated as a substitute for professional medical advice; always consult a medical practitioner. Any use of information in this book is at the reader's discretion and risk. Neither the author nor the publisher can be held responsible for any loss, claim or damage arising out of the use, or misuse, of the suggestions made, the failure to take medical advice or for any material on third party websites.

A catalogue record for this book is available from the British Library.

ISBN: 978-1-78180-115-4

Printed and bound in Great Britain by TJ International, Padstow, Cornwall.

For my mother, Phyllis Haner,
who saw the world through artist's eyes and
who taught me how to see the patterns all around us.

CONTENTS

"Then it was as if I suddenly saw the secret beauty of their hearts, the depths of their hearts where neither sin nor desire . . . can reach, the core of their reality; the person that each one is in the eyes of the Divine. If only they could all see themselves as they really are. If only we could see each other that way all of the time. There would be no more war, no more hatred, no more cruelty, no more greed . . . I suppose the big problem would be that we would fall down and worship each other."

— THOMAS MERTON

INTRODUCTION

Call me silly, but I never cease to marvel that Louise Hay is my friend. As author of the international bestseller *You Can Heal Your Life* and founder of Hay House, she's beloved by millions of people around the world. And she's even more wonderful than you probably imagine. Whether we're taking a walk through the wildflowers of Southern California, traveling to some far-flung location, or laughing over a meal together, being with her is just a pure joy and delight.

Over the past few years, we'd sometimes talked about how we felt that we had a destiny together. But I never expected that a simple Christmas gift from her would actually reveal one aspect of that destiny: the surprise discovery that her affirmations are validated by Chinese medicine, which is what my own work is based on, and the manifestation of this book.

I remember it was one of those magical winter nights when the air is crisp and clear and the darkness seems to sparkle. Louise had cooked an amazing soup made from vegetables grown in her garden; it was so rich with love and nutrients, each taste was powerful medicine. We spread organic butter on bread and enjoyed a beautiful salad as we laughed and talked. As the evening came to an end and I headed out the door, Louise handed me her new calendar of affirmations for the upcoming year.

As soon as I got home, I sat down to look through the calendar, admiring the power of the deceptively simple affirmations. I could feel my energy changing as I read them, and I thought, *Wow, imagine if everyone in the world would just read one of these every day!*

I kept turning the pages, reading one affirmation after the other, just soaking in their healing energy. But as I read, it dawned on me that I noticed patterns in their messages. In fact, what was becoming clear was that each affirmation fit like a perfect puzzle piece into each aspect of what Chinese medicine teaches about the human spirit. I sat straight up in my chair—was this my imagination?

I ended up pulling the pages from the calendar and sorting them according to the patterns I knew so well. My mouth hung open as I ended up with neat stacks of the same size, each applying to one classic personality type, emotional challenge, and phase of time in the human life cycle. It was a complete and coherent match to how Chinese medicine treats and transforms people's energy.

Chinese medicine is thousands of years old, and through century upon century of research, its creators and practitioners came to develop a very sophisticated understanding of how all life on Earth works. It's like a map of how energy moves in a complex but perfect symmetry of harmonious and balanced proportions. You can place this map over anything to see whether it's in coherence. Acupuncturists use this chart to diagnose your physical well-being, but it can also be applied to any situation—to evaluate whether a business plan is complete or how a romance is proceeding, and most important, to see the patterns in your own personality and how the design of your life is unfolding.

I sometimes use this map to evaluate another teacher's work, to see if it's whole or if there's anything missing in that particular system. But I'd never seen such a stunningly beautiful completion as I did that night, with Louise's affirmations spread around me. And so *The Hidden Symmetry of Your Birth Date* began to be born.

The purpose of this book is to help you discover how this energetic map uncovers the design concealed in your birth date, which is the hidden symmetry of your true spirit, and how to create a life in alignment with that design. Since your birth date not only reveals your inner nature, but the map for your whole life journey as well, this book will also guide you through every phase and year of your life in perfect harmony. Even if you feel you've lost your way, you can use this book to navigate back on course. It's never too late.

In Part I, you'll find how the timing of your birth influenced your overall personality, emotional self, and outer nature; as well as what you really need to be happy, your strengths and challenges in relationships, and your true calling in life. We'll conclude with Louise's affirmations that specifically support each of the nine personality types.

In Part II, we'll turn to look at how you move through your own personal seasons and how you can ride the waves of time rather than "push the river." You'll discover the four important transitions in life, as well as the meaning and purpose of each decade and each individual year of your past, present, and future. This section concludes with powerful affirmations from Louise to help you align with the energy of any year you're in.

Part III gives us a fascinating look at how Louise has embraced her own hidden symmetry to create a life of balance and flow, and how you can, too!

A Note about Pronouns

In this book, in order to avoid awkward "he/she" or "him/her" references, I prefer to use the neutral pronoun "they." Interestingly, this was an accepted universal pronoun in the English language as early as the time of Chaucer, used for masculine and feminine, singular and plural. This fell out of favor in the 18th century, when the new rule was that "he" should be used for both men and women, and that certainly doesn't seem to fit our times.

PART I

HOW TIME AFFECTS WHO YOU ARE

*"I want to sing like the birds sing,
not worrying about who
hears or what they think."*

— ATTRIBUTED TO JALAL AL-DIN RUMI

CHAPTER 1

THE DAY YOU WERE BORN

All this spring, a bird sang outside my window. It began with the first stirrings of each dawn, and then that tiny bird sang with gusto through all the hours of the day, for weeks on end. You'd think it would be annoying to have that endless background music, but I loved it. It was a beautiful and intricate song, full of spiraling trills, but what was most fascinating was how clearly insistent it was. That bird believed its song with every cell in its body; it sang with its whole heart and soul, the truth of its being. It was obvious that it couldn't not sing—it was purely and wholly involved in the rightness of the theme song for this time in its life.

As spring phased into summer, the birdsong trailed off and then disappeared. I guess it had been a courting melody, driven by the urgency to reproduce and continue the species. Maybe the bird went on to sing different notes as it was tending eggs, feeding chirping babies, teaching them how to fly, and then moving on to whatever was the next phase of its birdie purpose and plan in life.

This is how it is with every creature in nature: a bird, a bunny, a moth, a flower, a microbe, and all living things. They're born with a unique purpose and plan, and they joyfully do what they're here to do, in the rhythm of when they're supposed to do it, without a doubt crossing their minds. Life just unfolds as it's meant to. All living things do this but one, it seems. We humans are born; and as we grow up, we start trying to "find" ourselves by walking around and bumping into walls.

What if, just as for every other living being, there's a harmonious design for who you're meant to be and a plan for what to do in any stage? How amazing would it be to see all the pieces come together in the jigsaw puzzle of your life so that you could become your true self and move through the years riding the waves rather than fighting the current?

The Chinese have a word for the ordering principle of the universe: *tao*. Usually translated as "the way," it is the nature of things, that invisible plan for how all life works. There's an elegant symmetry to this way of being, a balance among its diverse movements that allows for all the gloriously juicy ways life takes form.

But you also have a personal tao, the hidden pattern of your true design and destiny. When you've experienced moments of synchronicity, you've had direct contact with your tao, attuned to your inner plan. What if you could always live in that kind of flow and sing your unique truth at every stage of your life with the same ease, vitality, and joy as that little bird? In the following pages, you'll find out how!

Symmetry

I sometimes imagine them, those ancient scientists thousands of years ago, striding across the Chinese landscape, observing how the shadows moved across the hills; the ways each plant sprouted, bloomed, and faded; how animals were born, thrived, and declined. In my mind, I see them note all the intricate ways each season was different, and how night moved into day, even how hour to hour of each day held a different quality. Over and over, they gazed up to survey how the stars move in their natural journey across the night skies throughout the year. They watched the people in their villages as they moved through their lives, each stage with a certain purpose and meaning, and studied all the various ways humans experience change over time.

Through the centuries of this kind of deep observation, these researchers developed a profound understanding of the patterns of nature, so subtly and intricately balanced, which are the foundation for all life on Earth, including human beings. And from this they created a sophisticated map of how everything on this planet works in perfect symmetry.

The word *symmetry* has different connotations. The first thing you may think of when you read that word is something that's exactly the same on one side as on the other, like a grade-school Valentine heart cut from folded paper. Yet in physics, symmetry is defined as "immunity to change"—in other words, that an experiment should give the same results no matter where or when it's performed. In fact, the concept of symmetry is considered so integral to the way life works that Albert Einstein used it as a fundamental principle when he developed his general theory of relativity, and it's believed to be the core of the "theory of everything" that physicists are currently searching for.

And there's yet another meaning for symmetry that signifies balanced and harmonious beauty of form, but doesn't necessarily imply that all the parts are perfect mirror images. There's a coherence to the form because of an inner order, an organizing principle. This is easily seen in the patterns of nature where there's a congruency, an orderliness in the design and function of any living thing, as well as in the cycles of the seasons, times of day, and phases of life experience.

All three kinds of symmetry actually apply to the meaning of your hidden design. Each of your personal characteristics has two sides to it just like that Valentine heart, one representing a strength and the other its corresponding challenge, and together they form the perfect whole. The definition of symmetry as immunity to change also fits, as your inner design is one from which we can reliably predict and understand every aspect of your personality; your thoughts, feelings, and behavior; and what you need to be happy in life. Your makeup never changes; although you may express its qualities in different ways as you go through your life, they're always rooted in the same meaning. And finally, in terms of balance and harmony of form, the patterns of your true nature have a coherent beauty to them, like your own personal mandala design.

Figure 1: The Yin Yang Symbol

The classic Chinese model of the universe, the yin yang symbol, is the essential representation of the symmetry of all life. Originally, the black half of the circle represented the shady side of the mountain that the sun hasn't yet warmed, so it is dark, cold, and wet with dew. And the white half of the circle related to the sunny side of the mountain, where it is bright, hot, and dry. But this is a map that reveals the duality of *all* things in nature. For example, yin is not only dark, cold, and wet; it also encompasses qualities such as stillness, silence, caution, night, winter, the moon, and feminine energy. Yang is not only bright, hot, and dry; it's also action, noise, confidence, day, summer, the sun, and masculine energy.

But nothing is totally yin or yang. Within each half of the circle, you see a dot that is its opposite. On the white half, there is a dot of black; on the black half, there is a dot of white. This represents the truth that within one is the seed of the other, day always turning into night, summer moving toward winter, and back again. The meaning infused in this simple circle is that all life is interconnected and interdependent, that everything is part of a balanced and dynamic system and interacts to form the greater whole.

This symbol is a deceptively simple design that the ancient Chinese further developed to uncover the intricacies in the symmetrical patterns of nature. These scientists became the first physicians, refining this into a map of how *qi* (which means "energy" or "life force") moves through the human body, and what to do when that flow is out of balance. Chinese medicine was the very first holistic medicine, recognizing that human anatomy is a tapestry of interconnected energy meridians and systems, with each part affecting and affected by the others in an invisible harmony.

This system is also used in feng shui to perceive the ways energy naturally travels through an environment and to understand how to direct it so that it positively affects the people in that place. And this same knowledge is used in Chinese face reading to see your inner design reflected in the patterns of your face and to know how to create a life in alignment with your unique nature.

As the Chinese studied and further refined this map, they also came to understand how energy moves through time. There are discernible patterns here—just as there are in everything—that deeply affect who you are overall and how you travel through your life. What they discovered over three millennia of "research and development" reveals your own inner makeup and the cycles you'll experience.

It's as if on the day you were born, you were imprinted by the patterns of energy that existed at that time, infusing your essence with their unique qualities to inform your inner spirit, what you came here to learn, and what your ultimate purpose will be.

At the same time, the map for your entire journey was formed. Like your own personal tide table—the ebbs and flows of your life—each phase of the invisible influence of time was set into motion on the day you were born. Just as with everything in nature, this design of your true self and your life plan have an intentional symmetry that's beautiful to behold.

Nine Star Ki

If you study the night sky over the years, you'll notice that the stars appear in different patterns according to the seasons. The Chinese observed that they could anticipate the specific cycles of each season by watching the movement of the stars, thus knowing when to prepare to plant, how to tend the fields, and to harvest the crops at just the right time. There were nine specific stars to which they paid particular attention, tracking them for guidance about the phases of time.

This research led to a system of understanding how time affects people's lives that's still based on the symmetry of yin and yang but is further evolved. It's called Nine Star Ki. The word *ki* (pronounced "key") is the Japanese word for the Chinese qi, which you'll recall means energy or life force. Ki is used instead of qi because in its journey through Asia to the West, this system most recently came from Japan.

Nine Star Ki is the study of how the patterns of energy move harmoniously through time. Although it has the word *star* in its name, it isn't astrology and has nothing to do with the movement of planets or stars affecting us. It's based on the study of natural cycles such as years; seasons; times of day; and the lives of plants, animals, and humans—every aspect of life on Earth.

Nine Star Ki is said to be the oldest form of understanding how the phases of time affect people; some say it originated in India 7,000 years ago, then moved through Tibet to China, where it was further developed over centuries. From there it eventually made its way to Japan, where that culture influenced it the way it has many other things—by refining it into a beautifully simple, elegant, and sophisticated system, without the superstition and gender bias of other Asian methods of guidance, such as Chinese astrology.

Nine Star Ki is barely known in the West, partly because it was an oral tradition, like most knowledge from ancient times in Asia. There was little in writing; instead the information was mostly spoken from master to student over the centuries. It was

introduced to the West in the 1960s by Japanese teachers Michio Kushi and Takashi Yoshikawa. The latter gained renown as the advisor to John Lennon and Yoko Ono, using Nine Star Ki to guide them on a regular basis. And with the rise in popularity of feng shui in the 1990s, this system received more attention because it shares the same foundation.

⌒

I often tell people I'm one of the more skeptical individuals they'll ever meet, and that's even true when it comes to the various methods of understanding the human spirit. I have a hard time accepting most systems created to evaluate personality types, because they're usually far too analytical and judgmental, all from the head and nothing from the heart, focused on creating new boxes to put people in so that we can feel more comfortable in our own little boxes. And a system devised by one person is very likely to be so heavily colored by their own personality and belief systems that I don't trust it to give a clear understanding of anyone aside from the inner workings of that individual's mind.

This is why I have such respect for the gifts Nine Star Ki has to offer us. This knowledge was developed over thousands of years, through many different researchers' study of nature. These observations were repeated over and over for centuries, honing and deepening the understanding of these universal principles, bequeathing to us an astonishingly elegant map of the human experience. And what could be more reliable than to trust nature, the system the Divine created?

In my work with Chinese face reading, which is based on the same understanding, I always give equal consideration to what I'm reading on someone's face *and* in their birth date, using Nine Star Ki. In order to fully understand anyone's true nature, I find it imperative to evaluate the meaning of both the timing of their birth and the design of the face they were born into. (You can learn to read your face with my other books: *The Wisdom of Your Face* and *The Wisdom of Your Child's Face*.)

In some cases, the information I see on someone's face and in their Nine Star Ki is similar, but often what I discover in their Nine Star Ki gives me strikingly different insights that open up new ways to understand that person on a very deep level and to know how to guide them to fully live their purpose and find happiness.

Of course your individual energetic "signature" is formed by many influences, including how you were raised by your parents and the unique experiences you've had. But as Chinese medicine teaches, everything is interconnected, and the imprint from the timing of your birth is swirling, mingling, and interacting with all these other influences. Who you are will affect how you perceive your parents' behavior toward you, and your reactions to all your life experiences will be influenced by your inherent personal patterns.

This system gives you an incredibly rich understanding of your hidden symmetry—the intricate design that makes you who you are and influences how your life unfolds. You can use this wisdom to discover how to tap into your core strengths, to find genuine intimacy in love, and to do your best work in the world. This knowledge reveals the harmonious theme running through all of your life challenges, as well as shows you what your true calling is meant to be and how to achieve it.

You can also use the system to discover the rhythm you're dancing to, the choreography of cycles you'll predictably move through all your life. With this understanding, you'll see why this particular year is bringing you the experiences you're having and how to make the best progress by aligning with that theme. You can anticipate what's coming next and prepare appropriately rather than be surprised by what shows up. You can even look back at the phases of time to discover the true meaning of a certain year's experience and why it happened the way it did.

Nine Star Ki empowers you to make major decisions and time important changes, to know how to go with the flow of any stage so that life can happen as effortlessly as possible. It's never too late to start to move through time in alignment with your own

true nature; and when you do, what comes to you is what you need in every moment. Then you can finally be in the right place at the right time.

So let's get started now, and discover the meanings and messages in the patterns of your own birth date!

CHAPTER 2

THIS IS NOT ABOUT NUMBERS

For decades, I've studied Chinese medicine and philosophy and what they teach us about the human spirit. But I've always been fascinated by what makes people tick and studied many other methods of understanding people, too, as well as energy and healing modalities that can help bring balance back to their lives. What I've found is that the more complicated a system is, the less mature it is. The more deeply developed and evolved teachings always seem to be elegantly and deceptively simple. Nine Star Ki is that kind of system. The first impression you may have is that it's so simple, you don't see how it could tell you very much. But that idea will soon disappear!

Nine Star Ki provides a kind of shorthand to let you easily and immediately grasp your inherent patterns of personality and the plan for your journey through life. This shorthand is expressed in numbers—you receive a set of three numbers that defines your true nature. But let me hasten to add something important: This is not numerology. Neither is this a method where you have to do calculations (so if you're math-phobic, you can now breathe again!).

Instead, the numbers are just streamlined terms to describe qualities of energy, symbols that reveal important aspects of your personal universe. Your first number represents your overall personality, who you showed up to be in this life. Your second number signifies your emotional self, and the feelings and behavior you revert to under stress. Your third number indicates how you do your work in the world, but also represents two other important things: the theme of the challenges you continually bump up against throughout life, and your ultimate purpose, the true calling that you achieve only by working through these challenges.

In these seemingly simple three numbers, you can discover how to align yourself with your unique inner plan, learn to fully love and accept yourself, attract healthy relationships, and achieve your fullest potential. And if you've ever wondered why your life is going the way it is, in these pages you'll discover the true rhythm of your personal journey and how to navigate on course from here.

The instructions that follow will show you how to discover your three-number pattern. These numbers are your personal Nine Star Ki, and you'll be using them as you work with the rest of this book. You can use the blank page at the very end of the book to record your numbers as well as the combinations for all the people in your life, past and present. I promise you'll have some astonishing "Aha!" moments regarding yourself and those who have been important to you, as well as the timing of important events or life experiences!

Using the Nine Star Ki Chart

Before you use the chart at the end of this chapter, there is something important you need to know: In this system, the calendar is slightly different. Instead of each year starting on January 1, a year is considered to begin on February 4. So, in other words, the year 2013 didn't begin on January 1, 2013; it began on February 4, 2013. Any date that falls before February 4 is considered to belong to the previous year instead.

This time frame has nothing to do with the date of Chinese New Year, which changes from year to year. Instead, the system is based on observation of the cycles of nature. February 4 is the midpoint between the solstice on December 21 and the equinox on March 21, and it was found over the centuries to be the natural starting place for the new year.

What this means for you is that if your birthday is from January 1 through February 3 of any particular year, in Nine Star Ki you were actually born the previous year. For instance, if you were born January 1, 1979, in this system, you were born January 1, 1978. If you were born January 23, 1954, with this system, you were born January 23, 1953. If you were born on February 3, 1988, you were born on February 3, 1987.

So when you refer to the chart, you'll need to keep this in mind. For any birth date that falls on January 1 through February 3, you have to go back one year. The month and day stay the same; only the year changes.

If you were born February 4 through December 31 of any particular year, you don't need to change anything. So if you were born February 4, 1967, that date stays the same: February 4, 1967. If you were born June 8, 1980, you were still born June 8, 1980!

How to Use the Chart

1. Find your birth year in the columns at the top of the page. (Keep in mind that if you were born January 1–February 3, your birth year is actually the prior year. See instructions in the preceding paragraphs.)

2. Find where the month and day of your birth fall in the rows at the left of the page.

3. Trace across the row until you come to the column your birth year is in. The set of three numbers you see there is your set of Nine Star Ki numbers.

Example: You were born March 13, 1969

- You find that the column with 1969 in it is the 4 column.

- You then see that March 13 falls within the dates March 6–April 5 at the left-hand side of the page.

- You follow that row over till you reach the 4 column and discover that your Nine Star Ki numbers are 4.7.2.

Example: You were born February 1, 1957

- Because that is before February 4, you change your birth date to February 1, 1956.

- Then you look at the columns at the top of the page to discover that 1956 falls in the 8 column.

- You then find that February 1 falls within the dates January 6–February 3 at the left-hand side of the page.

- You follow that row over till you reach the 8 column and discover that your Nine Star Ki numbers are 8.9.4.

Example: You were born December 31, 1977

- You find the column with 1977 in it is the 5 column.

- You then see that December 31 falls within the dates December 8–January 5 at the left-hand side of the page.

- You follow that row over till you reach the 5 column and discover that your Nine Star Ki numbers are 5.1.9.

For Dates Not Listed on the Chart

You can use the chart at the end of the chapter to quickly find the Nine Star Ki numbers for people born in the 20th century and the beginning of the 21st, but if you want to research someone born prior to or after that time, here's an easy way to do it:

1. Add up the numbers in their birth year until you're left with a single digit.

For example, for someone born in 1887, you'd add 1 + 8 + 8 + 7, to get 24. Then you'd add the 2 + 4 to come up with a single digit, so the final number would be 6.

2. Subtract that single digit from 11.

When you added 1887, you ended up with 6. If you subtract 6 from 11, you get 5.

3. The number you end up with is the first of that person's Nine Star Ki numbers. You'd then locate the column with that number in it on the chart.

For example, for 1887, your calculation brought you to the number 5. So you'd look in the 5 column in the chart.

4. Then you simply find where the month and day of their birth falls in the rows at the left of the chart, as you've done with all the other birth dates.

For example, someone born on June 23, 1887, was a 5.7.3.

(Keep in mind, however, that anyone born from January 1–February 3 is considered to have been born the previous year. So a birth date of January 9, 1773, would become January 9, 1772.)

Nine Star Ki Chart

Before using this chart, please read the instructions that appear earlier in the chapter: "Using the Nine Star Ki Chart."
(REMINDER: Any birthday from Jan. 1 through Feb. 3 is considered to be in the previous year.)

	9	8	7	6	5	4	3	2	1
	1901	1902	1903	1904	1905	1906	1907	1908	1909
	1910	1911	1912	1913	1914	1915	1916	1917	1918
	1919	1920	1921	1922	1923	1924	1925	1926	1927
	1928	1929	1930	1931	1932	1933	1934	1935	1936
	1937	1938	1939	1940	1941	1942	1943	1944	1945
	1946	1947	1948	1949	1950	1951	1952	1953	1954
	1955	1956	1957	1958	1959	1960	1961	1962	1963
	1964	1965	1966	1967	1968	1969	1970	1971	1972
	1973	1974	1975	1976	1977	1978	1979	1980	1981
	1982	1983	1984	1985	1986	1987	1988	1989	1990
	1991	1992	1993	1994	1995	1996	1997	1998	1999
	2000	2001	2002	2003	2004	2005	2006	2007	2008
	2009	2010	2011	2012	2013	2014	2015	2016	2017
	2018	2019	2020	2021	2022	2023	2024	2025	2026
	2027	2028	2029	2030	2031	2032	2033	2034	2035
	9	**8**	**7**	**6**	**5**	**4**	**3**	**2**	**1**
Feb. 4–March 5	9.5.9	8.2.2	7.8.4	6.5.6	5.2.8	4.8.1	3.5.3	2.2.5	1.8.7
March 6–April 5	9.4.1	8.1.3	7.7.5	6.4.7	5.1.9	4.7.2	3.4.4	2.1.6	1.7.8
April 6–May 5	9.3.2	8.9.4	7.6.6	6.3.8	5.9.1	4.6.3	3.3.5	2.9.7	1.6.9
May 6–June 5	9.2.3	8.8.5	7.5.7	6.2.9	5.8.2	4.5.4	3.2.6	2.8.8	1.5.1
June 6–July 7	9.1.4	8.7.6	7.4.8	6.1.1	5.7.3	4.4.5	3.1.7	2.7.9	1.4.2
July 8–Aug. 7	9.9.5	8.6.7	7.3.9	6.9.2	5.6.4	4.3.6	3.9.8	2.6.1	1.3.3
Aug. 8–Sept. 7	9.8.6	8.5.8	7.2.1	6.8.3	5.5.5	4.2.7	3.8.9	2.5.2	1.2.4
Sept. 8–Oct. 8	9.7.7	8.4.9	7.1.2	6.7.4	5.4.6	4.1.8	3.7.1	2.4.3	1.1.5
Oct. 9–Nov. 7	9.6.8	8.3.1	7.9.3	6.6.5	5.3.7	4.9.9	3.6.2	2.3.4	1.9.6
Nov. 8–Dec. 7	9.5.9	8.2.2	7.8.4	6.5.6	5.2.8	4.8.1	3.5.3	2.2.5	1.8.7
Dec. 8–Jan. 5	9.4.1	8.1.3	7.7.5	6.4.7	5.1.9	4.7.2	3.4.4	2.1.6	1.7.8
Jan. 6–Feb. 3	9.3.2	8.9.4	7.6.6	6.3.8	5.9.1	4.6.3	3.3.5	2.9.7	1.6.9

CHAPTER 3

YOUR MAIN
PERSONALITY

Now that you know what your three numbers are, it's time to begin your journey into your own unique nature. In this chapter, you'll start by exploring the meaning of your first number. In other words, if your numbers are 2.1.6, you'll be paying attention to the section below that describes the Two personality.

Your first number reveals your overall personality; what you tend to think about as you go through your day; what you value; your patterns of perception; and your needs in terms of lifestyle, relationships, and life in general.

Note: The main personality of anyone who is under the age of 18 is considered to be heavily influenced by their second number as well as their first. This is because the second number reflects the emotional self, almost like the inner child. When someone is still a minor, they live as much in their child nature as their main one, so if you're evaluating someone under 18, some of their personality may seem more like their second number than their first. To understand them at this stage, my advice is to read the description for their first number and then read the description for their second number as if it were their first. You may see aspects of that second number in who they are now, but you can know that the first number is who they're maturing into.

What follows are thorough descriptions of each of the first numbers.

First Number: One
Innovator

Your innovative mind allows you to come up with ideas and solutions to problems in unusual ways, drawing much more from your creative nature and instinctive sense of things rather than any linear, logical way of thinking. People may often be amazed by how you got that brilliant idea, and you'll have no way of explaining your thought process, because it really isn't about thinking—it's more of an inner knowing. You're definitely intuitive; it's almost as though you have lines of communication with other realms and can download wisdom and insights in mysterious ways.

The image in nature for the One is water, and there's definitely a flow to your energy. You don't do things in straight lines, and this means you can be quite adaptable; but you are not a clock-watcher and may often run late as a result. People will need to understand this isn't deliberate on your part!

Inner Depth

As part of this characteristic flow, you'll tend to process things slowly, work out any decision over time, or make life changes gradually. Others may say you wait too long to get going, but what they don't realize is that you're working through everything deep inside and this takes time. However, it's also true that you can tread water for *too* long and miss opportunities. It's important to evaluate whether there's a legitimate reason for continuing to float, or if fear is blocking you from moving forward.

As a One, you're like an iceberg: What others see is only the tiny tip; everything is happening under the surface. On one hand, this gives you a mysterious charm that people can find intriguing and magnetically attractive. But you may not easily show your feelings, or may keep what you're thinking to yourself, and you can feel overwhelmed if someone is chattering on and on or speaking too quickly and pushing you to respond just as

fast. You may hide what you're uncomfortable about in a relation-ship rather than talk about it; and at the extreme, you can keep secrets from your partner. You won't think of it as being secretive, though; you're just afraid to bring up things that might upset the other person. But you can tend to choose secrecy or withholding information in situations when that's not a good decision.

Privacy and quiet time will be important to you, when you can sink in and just "be" for a while. You may prefer environ-ments with mood lighting instead of a glaringly bright room; and you might love to be horizontal, lying in bed to work or stretch-ing out in a nice warm bath at the end of the day.

You have a deep inner willpower that gives you the strength to push through difficult times with an impressive tenacity and determination. This same strong will also translates to a healthy stubbornness, which can serve you well by giving you the abil-ity to say no when you don't want to do something or to move forward despite all odds. But it also creates the potential for you to become obstinate or inflexible, and sometimes people may say you're being stubborn when you think that you're just sticking to your guns!

Emotional Process

One of the most important things to understand as a One is that you feel things more deeply than others do. You're more in touch with your emotions than most people are; it could be said that you process *life* emotionally. But you're not overt about your feelings—they're often hidden and not expressed. Tears may eas-ily well up in your eyes, but you're usually not one to burst into sobs in front of someone. You may worry that others could judge you as weak or overly emotional if you do show what you feel. In fact, you actually have enormous strength, and this is what allows you to have such profound emotions.

One common experience may be that your feelings can be easily hurt. There's a lot going on deep inside that's not visible to others: on the outside, you can seem calm, quiet, and strong, which gives people the impression that anything they say or do will just roll right off your back. Nothing could be further from the truth, however. If someone does something hurtful, it can be like a knife in your heart. If this happens, you'll probably clam up, fall silent as if you've lost your voice, and withdraw, unable to talk it out to resolve things with them. In this situation, you can too easily experience a loss of trust to one degree or another.

These kinds of situations are often due to a mutual misunderstanding. The other person didn't intend to hurt you, but that's what it seemed like to you. Their behavior may have been a consequence of seeing your calm exterior and underestimating the impact of their words or actions. If you can recognize this, it can help you move past the hurt.

The Influence of Fear

Although your tendency to pull back from others doesn't always serve you well, at times this behavior stems from a natural emotion that will be a frequent companion in your life: fear. Anyone whose first number is One will be familiar with this feeling, from fear of moving forward in life all the way down to a sense of cold, primal terror—fear about even surviving, financially, emotionally, or physically.

There's nothing wrong with fear. It's actually a healthy impulse and necessary to evaluate the risk in any situation. But for you, it can sometimes be a paralyzing influence. The advice to "feel the fear and do it anyway" can be useful once you realize what's keeping you stuck.

Ones sometimes struggle with issues of abandonment, which also come from fear—the fear of being left alone. You may too easily fall into perceiving an experience as having been abandoned or ostracized, whether that's behavior by a colleague in a staff meeting, a friend's actions at a party, or a lover's choices in romance. You could at times have a pattern of thinking people

are leaving you out; while other times, it may just be a sense that you're different from everyone else. Once you can recognize when these feelings are coming up, you can catch yourself before you get swept away by emotions that may be based less on reality than on fear.

What I've observed about human beings is that we all think everyone else is like us—or should be! If you're a One, it's your nature to have a lot going on under the surface and to not communicate everything that you're thinking or feeling. Because of this, it's likely that you believe other people usually don't say everything that's going on inside either. Then your creative mind takes over, and you may start to fantasize about what the other person is really thinking but not saying. This can lead you to make assumptions that aren't at all true or even to become fearful that the other person is keeping secrets from *you*.

With some Ones, this can flood their life. They may believe that others are talking about them or plotting against them, or at the extreme, become paranoid and obsessed with things like conspiracy theories. One man quit his job because he thought the company was bugging his phone. The reality was that there'd been a glitch in the telephone system as it was being repaired, and someone ended up sharing his line.

Ancestors

An interesting aspect of being a One has to do with what the Chinese call *ancestors*. Now when we hear this word in Western culture, we may think of our great-great-grandparents or our forebears emigrating from their country of origin.

But in China, the term has a richer meaning. When an elder dies and passes on, it's believed they become an ancestor who continues to beam blessings onto the family, offering their wisdom and strength from that point on. This is how feng shui originated: to determine where to locate Grandfather's grave so that his blessings would be directed to your house instead of the neighbor's by mistake!

This energy offered from our ancestors is deep and powerful, and it's important for all of us to tap into it as a source of profound support in life. But instead, most of us labor under the illusion that it's up to us to tough things out and "make" everything happen in our lives. If only we knew that our ancestors stand behind us, offering infinite help for us at all times.

In the body, the kidneys represent the essence of the ancestors. You have two kidneys, one on each side of your back; and they can be imagined as the two hands of your ancestors, supporting you and letting you lean on them. Feel their deep strength flood into your system instead of having to power through life draining your own will.

This is important for all of us to know; but for a One, there's an especially strong connection to your ancestors, and you need to make use of the blessings you receive from the other side. It can even be as if you've inherited gifts down through your family line, talents or traits that you should accept and use in order to find true happiness in life.

If you're a One, give some thought to any special quality you may have inherited, whether that's Grandfather's musical talent or an interest in chemistry like Great-Aunt Mary. If you've tended to look at it as just a distraction and a waste of time, you could be mistaken. You may or may not earn a living with this gift, but it's essential that you allow the inheritance to be active in your life.

Another way that you can understand this issue is that as a One, you can also have spiritual ancestors who have nothing to do with your bloodline or family of origin. Instead, it's as if you have guides or wise ones on the other side from whom you can draw power and wisdom. For example, your naturally strong intuitive abilities come from your tapping into this other world. The more you allow this connection to your ancestors, the more easily you'll move into your strength in life.

Careers

To determine the types of careers that align with your inner design, we need to consider the influence of both your first and third numbers, so be sure to read the description of your calling in Chapter 5 as well.

No matter what kind of career you choose, you definitely need freedom in how you do your work, so being cooped up in an office or having to punch a time clock will smother your spirit. Jobs that let you be out "in the field" for much of the day or hours that aren't the standard nine to five can benefit you. You may be attracted to jobs that involve adventure and some risk as well— Ones can be found working with disaster-relief organizations such as FEMA.

Ones are often in the creative arts, especially music, but your innovative mind can also find success in finance, science, or medicine. You shouldn't ignore your intuitive abilities either, whether you earn a living as a psychic or more subtly rely on your gut instincts in whatever you do. Careers dealing with death and dying might interest you, including end-of-life counselor, funeral director, or genealogist.

It's also possible that your work will involve travel or living in exotic places, or have to do with water in some way. Mystery and magic can be a part of your life; for instance, you may write mystery novels, perform magic tricks, or be drawn to follow a guru or do shamanistic work.

First Number: Two
Mother

Your sweet generosity of spirit is one of your greatest strengths, and you're exceptionally kind and thoughtful in dealing with others. Like the archetypal Mother, whose first thought is always about taking care of her family, your attention will be directed toward how you can help someone else. People may keep turning to you for support or advice because they sense your sincere and caring nature, and because they know they can depend on you.

They're right. You are indeed very responsible, but this sense of responsibility can sometimes turn into the weight of feeling obligated, which can be a problem. If someone asks you to do something you just don't have time for, there's a chance you'll feel too guilty to say no and will do it even if it inconveniences you. It can be too easy to get caught up in a cycle of sacrificing your own needs while you take care of everyone else's.

It can be helpful to imagine a stereotypical mother in order to understand how Twos think and behave. Envision a mom falling into bed at midnight, exhausted after having just finished the laundry, her paperwork from the office, and making everyone's lunches for the next day. But if the baby cries at 2 A.M., who gets up? Mother. So Twos can have boundary issues—always working and never taking time for themselves or being so other-directed in their lives that at the extreme, they can lose all sense of themselves.

Devotion to Others

This issue can be exacerbated by how important family, friends, and relationships are to you. If only you didn't care so much, you could set stronger boundaries! But you're a true-blue friend and the thought of *not* being there for someone seems inconceivable. You can so easily forget the importance of your own needs, but good self-care is essential in order for a Two to stay healthy physically and emotionally. If you wear yourself out, how can you continue to be there for those you love?

Twos are the peacemakers; they're upset by conflict and will set their needs aside, offer compromises, or try to placate everyone just to keep the peace. They're incredibly patient and loyal, but if things go wrong, a Two can be a doormat in a relationship or stay far beyond the time anyone else would have left. Even if their partner is abusive, they may stay because they feel sorry for him or her and believe the apologies and promises to change. Or their concerns will be for the children, and they try to wait until the kids leave home before claiming their freedom.

Twos are naturally frugal with their money and tend to build a nest egg over time, but aren't attracted to taking financial risks in the hopes of hitting it big. If they do have substantial success with money, it's usually because they've partnered up with someone else who's more ambitious or demanding.

One of the most important things to understand about your inner nature is your need to feel devoted to something. There's a strong desire to be of service, whether that's in devotion to family, career, or a cause. The theme of helping others comes up strongly here, and Twos are often driven to help in any situation, especially in providing kindness and comfort to others. Quan Yin, the Chinese goddess of compassion, is the epitome of what a Two can become, modeling a loving presence in any situation.

The Influence of Worry

The emotion that's a frequent companion for Twos is worry. Imagine Mother worrying about her family: Did her daughter do her homework? Has her son's cold turned into bronchitis? Will her husband deal with the problem with the in-laws? Did her assistant finish that important project, and why was her boss in such a bad mood today? The thoughts go around and around in her head and there's just no end.

As a Two, you worry so much because you care so much, but this tendency doesn't serve you well. As the worries repeatedly spin around in your brain, your mind becomes clogged and this keeps you from thinking clearly. So the result is that if there really *is* something to worry about, you're less able to think through how to deal with the situation. One way you can cope is to keep lists, because when you write something down, then you don't have to carry it in your head and there's less chance of mental congestion.

Like Mother, Twos are modest and humble; in fact, they usually believe that they're not creative or aren't very capable of coming up with original ideas. Instead, they feel unsure of themselves (again, the influence of worry), can be dependent on others, and may end up supporting someone else's success while they cheer from the sidelines.

However, there's one important factor here. If you're a Two, it's said that for the first half of your life, you succeed by supporting others. But in the middle of your life, a shift happens and you have the opportunity to step into your power, to surpass everyone you ever supported. Louise Hay, a Two, is a shining example of this achievement, as she first emerged as a great teacher in her early 50s and founded Hay House as she turned 60.

Home, Family, and Friends

For Mother, home is the most important place, and her favorite activity is to feed her family. You may feel most joyful when everyone you love is gathered at home to celebrate holiday meals together. You can be sentimental, with photos of family and friends placed throughout the house, and you tend to cherish every gift anyone has ever given you. This can sometimes cause a problem with clutter!

Twos always feel a need to go through life arm in arm with someone, personally and professionally. Heidi, a Two, made a new friend who shared her love of thrift stores and soon they become inseparable. She was in heaven because her need for companionship was finally fulfilled. Then her friend came down with a terrible cold one day and called to say she was going to stay home. What did Heidi do? She cooked up a big pot of homemade soup and carried it over to her friend's house.

But her friend was one of those people who wanted to be left *alone* when ill, and she refused to answer the front door. Heidi went around to the back door and knocked and knocked and called on the phone. Even after she forlornly returned home,

she phoned incessantly over the next two days, leaving messages to say that she'd be happy to bring her friend food, take care of her, and keep her company. To Heidi, this was a show of love and friendship. But the other woman interpreted this as a serious boundary violation; and when she finally returned the calls, it was to tell Heidi to never contact her again. The friendship was over.

To others, sometimes Twos can appear needy or clingy—and some can be. In their minds, if you love someone, why would you ever not want to be with them? These are simply different perceptions and ways of being in the world; but without understanding, they can create stress in relationships.

Balance Giving with Receiving

With such a maternal theme imprinted in their nature, Twos are often very sweet and selfless, with a genuine devotion to helping others. But sometimes Mother can become negative. If you picture the stereotypical mom, always working to take care of the family and thinking of all the special ways she can make them feel happy and loved, what can easily happen is that she sets her needs aside far too often. In fact, she may be spending all of her time taking care of others—driving the kids to various activities, picking up after her husband, and covering for her boss so that she has to cancel that appointment for the first massage she's had in a year.

Somewhere in the back of Mother's mind, there can be an expectation that surely, eventually, the family will return the love by also doing some sweet and thoughtful things for her—but this doesn't happen. The family is supposed to be taken care of by Mother, not the other way around! So they take her for granted and continue to make demands and take advantage of her. Over time, she can develop a growing sense of disappointment that may eventually turn into resentment. *After all I've done for you, this is what I get?* is the feeling that gets stuck in her mind.

Whether or not they're parents—or even if they don't spend a lot of time helping others—Twos can too easily develop a kind of victim mentality, a "poor me" tape running through their heads. They may keep feeling sorry for themselves or act like martyrs. Other times, Twos can turn resentful and angry, the stereotypical "I spent 36 hours in labor but you never call me?" attitude. Then nothing anyone does is right. The Two has become unreceptive and isn't even able to recognize or accept others' efforts. Fortunately, it's rare for things to get this extreme.

At the heart of this issue is the fact that Twos are driven to give, even to the point of giving away their power. Deep inside, they really don't feel powerful, and believe no one is there to help them. Part of their desire to take care of others comes from a deep need to be *taken care of.* The unconscious hope is that if they help someone else, then that person will step up to provide for them in return. But as I've described, this doesn't always happen. Instead, others accept help but don't have as strong a sense of responsibility to give back—or at least not in the way the Two thinks they need.

If you're a Two, be mindful of how you may even subtly click into some version of that "poor me" story in any situation. If you do, the cure is to attend to building your own boundaries and personal power, to know with all certainty that you're completely equipped to be in charge of your life.

It can take a while to reverse a decades-long pattern of over-giving, including relinquishing your power. It's important to understand that the process of giving is actually only half of a full cycle, and you also need to learn how to open your arms and *receive* in return. Sometimes that even means you need to (horrors!) *ask for* and accept help.

Remember that life loves you, and you can rest in the trust that as you build your receptivity muscles, more support will flood in!

Careers

To determine the types of careers that align with your inner design, we need to consider the influence of both your first and third numbers, so be sure to read the description of your calling in Chapter 5 as well.

Whatever your work, you're great at making sure things get done, and you can stay with a project until it's complete when others would give up in frustration. Twos often work in support positions, or else they're the person everyone comes to for help or advice, even if the job description has nothing to do with support. Twos can excel as managers as well because they balance the needs of both the company and the staff to create a win-win situation.

Twos make excellent teachers because they're so thoughtful about how to provide information in the way their students need to receive it. Other possible careers include real estate, the hospitality industry, nutrition, or food services. Because of their inherent pattern of caring for people, jobs in social work, nursing, psychology, or caregiving can be good choices. But remember the earlier advice that everything can change in midlife for a Two, and they can move into a position of power, no matter what their career.

First Number: Three
Warrior

Enthusiastic and driven, you're the most active of all the personalities. In nature, this energy is represented by the vitality of early spring, when plants' drive to be alive is so powerful that little green sprouts can break through solid concrete. Your personality has that same spirit, which I call the Warrior—strong, fierce, and ready to launch into action. In fact, you're always on the go. You love to work, you love to be active, and you love to get things done! We'll never find you lounging on the couch eating bonbons; you value *doing* rather than *being*.

As a Three, you use your linear and logical mind to decide what the goal should be in any situation and devise a plan to achieve it as efficiently as possible. You're practical, pragmatic, and enjoy strategizing. You're the person we want if we're at point A and want to get to point Z in a straight line. In fact, once you come up with that plan, you'll want to leap into action to get to the finish line as fast as possible; it can be incredibly frustrating if you have to work with people who mill around at the starting gate still talking and going around in circles!

You have a very creative mind, but you want to do something tangible with your ideas, to make them real in the world in some way. For this reason, it may be enjoyable for you to build or design things, or in some way to see visible results of your work. In conversation, you tend to be direct and don't enjoy long discussions about a problem. You want to cut to the chase and figure out what's wrong and how to fix it—and then fix it!

Inner Tension

You'll thrive in situations where you can work on short-term projects that have discernible steps—or at least a beginning, middle, and end—and then let you move on to the next thing. It will be frustrating for you if something is overly complicated or drags on and on, and you may lose patience and give up. There can be a twitchiness about this Three energy. You may be impulsive and run with an idea rather than sit down and work through the details to be sure you have your ducks in a row. Threes are more likely than most of the other types to have impulse-control problems or attention disorders like ADD/ADHD.

While Threes can have a laser-like focus that allows them to concentrate intensely for short periods of time, it's also possible for them to develop a compulsive hyper-focus; for instance, playing computer games for hours on end. Both the twitchiness and the hyper-focus are due to a strong inner tension that feeds their tremendous drive in life, but it can result in behavior such as being a workaholic or struggling with other addictive tendencies. This inner tension can prevent them from ever really relaxing; instead they have a go-go-go way of living. It's important for Threes to find ways to blow off steam, to release some of this tension, and to create more of a balance that includes both activity and downtime.

If this sounds like you, don't despair. Fortunately, you also hold the key to dealing with these problems since you have an inherently strong sense of discipline that empowers you to take charge and create boundaries for your behavior. For instance, Laurie was a Three who had a problem with compulsive cleaning. After working all day, she couldn't relax with her family. Instead, as soon as dinner was over, she started cleaning and couldn't stop. Her husband had to force her to go to bed each night. Laurie finally worked up a structured schedule that included a morning run and 20 minutes of strength-training exercises each evening. When she stuck to this system religiously, things improved drastically; she even found that there were some days when she didn't have to clean at all.

Regular physical exercise is always essential for Threes, especially if it can be done out in nature, which is very nourishing for their personal energy. When a Three is tired or stressed, being outdoors is better than taking a nap.

What's Next?

You're naturally optimistic and confident, with a sense that no matter what happens, you can figure out how to handle it. You have a "let's move on" outlook on life and are always looking for what's next, expecting that some interesting new opportunity is right around the corner. And as part of this characteristic, you'll be a lifelong student, always wanting to learn, grow, and change.

Yet because of this natural desire to move forward, you may sometimes be perceived as pushy or aggressive. You're not wishy-washy—you know what you want and you know how to get it, and if someone is in your way, it's possible that you may try to inappropriately push. Being very direct, you can speak before you think, blurting out what's on your mind without regard for how it might make the other person feel; and you may not realize it if you've been too blunt or hurt their feelings. To you, it's just obvious what needs to be said or done, and you can't understand why people are so touchy!

One Three described herself as valuing "kitchen-table talks" in her relationship, where she and her boyfriend just sat down and talked a problem out until they reached a resolution. But he had a very different personality and viewed this as far too confrontational. He would become upset, feeling as if he were being challenged and put on the spot. Neither person was right or wrong; they were just seeing things through two different filters. Discovering what their birth dates revealed opened new options for them to communicate in ways that were a better fit.

Threes are said to have good vision—in other words, you can easily size up a problem and see a solution. And you can size up a person quickly as well. As soon as someone walks in the room, you make some decisions about who they are and what they're capable of. You're often very accurate in your ability to "see," but this tendency can also incline you to be judgmental, and you risk jumping to conclusions, making up your mind too quickly about someone.

You can be a natural rebel—challenging the status quo, questioning the rules, and resisting authority—and you may have a skeptical nature overall. You won't believe something just because someone said so, and they may have to work hard to convince you of the validity of their statement.

Most Threes love to challenge people in any interaction and actually enjoy an argument—but they think of it as a discussion! Some Threes seem to turn even the most innocuous conversation into a debate they have to win.

The Influence of Anger

The emotion that's imprinted in a Three's nature is anger. This can range from feeling mild irritation or impatience to frustration or indignation, and at the far end of the spectrum, full-out rage. In nature, the image for anger is thunder, and a big thunderclap is what a Three's anger often resembles—they shout, swear, bang, or break things. Then it's over, and they feel much better!

In our culture, we judge anger as a negative emotion; yet when you trace it back to its root cause, it's actually just a desire to create change. This can be a healthy impulse, such as wanting to stop someone from being mistreated or to break up old ways of doing things that are no longer working. The energy at the core of anger is a driving force that makes us move to change and grow; it's the booster rocket that launches us toward our goal.

Since we usually see anger expressed in unhealthy and destructive ways in everyday life, we judge it as bad and try to resist or suppress it when we feel it rising. However, this is often the very reason anger shows up in such a negative way. Suppression can only succeed for so long, and the energy of anger can become toxic as it's held inside. So when the emotion is finally released, it's then expressed in a harmful way, which can create a kind of vicious circle. A Three may immediately feel ashamed of their behavior and go back to trying to suppress it. Or the person who was the target of the angry outburst may respond in kind, and then they have a cycle of anger going back and forth between them and building on itself.

Threes need to feel in charge of their own lives, and when someone else has power over them, they can feel extremely uncomfortable. As part of this pattern, a hot button for this number is the issue of feeling dominated. For example, if a Three gets pulled over by the police, it can be really upsetting. They may show a chip-on-the-shoulder attitude that gets them in trouble, or it may take all their willpower to submit to the more powerful person without talking back.

In life in general, Threes are too likely to perceive others as trying to shame, blame, or dominate them even if that's not the case, and their reactions can bewilder the other person. One everyday example of this is that you'll rarely hear a Three genuinely say, "I'm sorry," or admit fault, even if they did make a mistake. If they only knew that for their partner, just finally hearing one simple apology might completely dissolve the bad feelings!

Transforming Anger

The worst thing that can happen is that as anger is held in, over time it can turn and be directed at the self instead of the person or event that provoked it. The result is depression. Even in Western psychology, this disorder is often defined as anger turned inward. To prevent or solve this situation, find a way to take action, to start the energy flowing out instead of inward. Exercise is a great way to change the direction of anger, shifting back out from the self. Another way is through work, especially volunteering or acting to help others in some way. And using the understanding of anger being thunder, making noise is another great way to get the energy moving out again. Think of drumming, shouting, or singing!

So the emotion of anger is bundled as part of your package as a Three. It's what creates your drive, your focus, and your desire to move forward in life. If you can tap into this emotion as a healthy force, it can have beneficial results. The most powerful use of your Warrior energy is to create positive change in the world, to right wrongs, and to make this a better place.

Careers

To determine the types of careers that align with your inner design, we need to consider the influence of both your first and third numbers, so be sure to read the description of your calling in Chapter 5 as well.

Because you're so driven, competitive, and goal oriented, you can succeed as an entrepreneur, but once the business is up and running, you may not be so good at managing it or keeping it going. Your attention naturally goes to the next idea rather than staying with what you've just brought to life, so it's best if you can put other people in place to take care of the day-to-day requirements. Then you don't feel locked into a mundane routine.

Threes can be successful attorneys because of their talent with preparing logical arguments and their competitive nature. Any career that has to do with thinking, analyzing, and planning can be fulfilling, such as architect, engineer, or analyst.

You love to be active, so a career in sports or as a personal trainer can be fulfilling; with your Warrior nature, work in the military or law enforcement is also attractive. Threes can enjoy politics as well because of their desire to make a difference. Other jobs that fit the Three nature are landscape designer, gardener, carpenter, or construction worker. Finally, you'd make an excellent personal coach because you're so good at strategy and you don't coddle people—you get them up off their rear ends and keep them going!

First Number: Four
Guide

One term used for the Four personality is the *gentle wind*. That kind of breeze blows in curves, not straight lines, so here we find personal characteristics of flexibility and an easygoing nature. Fours are said to be natural counselors because they're gentle and receptive to others and able to guide them in an open-minded and nonjudgmental manner.

Another image for this personality is that of the bamboo, a plant that is flexible and bends as the breeze blows, easily adjusting to changing conditions. If you're a Four, one of your greatest strengths is how adaptable you are, including your ability to deal with a wide variety of personality types. Things don't always have to be your way—you can see the point someone else is trying to make and can find a way to accommodate their needs. Fours are consistently described as gracious and kind, and people tend to like them immediately on first meeting.

Changeability

You have a logical mind and excellent common sense, and this serves you especially well in terms of planning and problem solving. You'll be able to create a good plan, but if you proceed and encounter obstacles, you'll be able to change to come up with a plan B. The theme of changeability pervades the Four nature, but sometimes in challenging ways. You can struggle with indecisiveness, never feeling sure of your decisions, choosing a direction and then backing off to rethink it, or wavering between options. And if that bamboo is buffeted by too much wind, it can whip back and forth until it finally splinters. This is how your mind can react when facing a complicated decision, getting flustered by too many choices and thinking not only of plan B, but also plans C, D, and on through J, ending up feeling totally confused.

Natalie, a Four, was going to meet two friends for dinner after work one day. Since she worked in the neighborhood where they were going to meet, she agreed to find a restaurant once she left the office and then call them to let them know where to go. But when they got Natalie's call, she was sitting on a bench on the street. The first place she went to was too crowded, at the second she didn't like the menu, the third had a long wait, the fourth was too expensive, and the fifth too cheap. At that point, she threw up her hands, wailing, "I can't decide!"

The bamboo has many branches spreading out from its trunk, and in just this way, your attention can go in many directions. At times there are so many things to consider and think about that you can find it hard to focus on just one. But this theme of distraction can affect you in other ways as well. For example, it's not unusual for Fours to be voracious readers of philosophy or how-to books but not do much with what they've learned. One woman had a floor-to-ceiling stack of self-help books by her bed; as soon as she finished one book, she'd immediately start another, but never put what she learned to use. She realized that she was actually using these books to keep herself distracted from deciding what she really wanted to do with her life.

The Influence of . . . Influence

One pattern that's strong in the Four nature centers around the concept of influence. For one thing, you can be easily influenced by others. Being so good at listening and adapting to those around you can affect your own process. If you're trying to make a decision, you'll hear what your friends have to say and if there are too many differing opinions, you'll feel even more uncertain. Or you'll make up your mind, but then your best friend will ask, *"Really?"* and you'll back off from your choice. If this happens too often, you can develop a feeling that you've been gullible and may become less trusting overall—not a good thing. Some Fours develop a strong natural skepticism and tend to doubt others' opinions or motives, and people often have to work hard to earn this number's trust. Some Fours take this too far and become overly judgmental and cynical.

But at the same time, you can be highly influential *for* other people. They'll listen to you because they sense you've thought things through and that you're not trying to push your own agenda. As a Four, you make a great mentor; but you'll also thrive if you have your own mentor or series of advisors to help guide you. You'll need to bounce ideas off individuals whose advice you feel you can trust.

Self-Judgment and Overthinking

As much as there's a potential to be judgmental about others, the worst of any judgment will be directed within: You can be extremely hard on yourself. The Four nature can keep you tensed up inside, upset with yourself over every little misstep. If you don't find ways to not judge yourself so harshly, this can become a self-destructive impulse, at worst causing a struggle with depression or addiction. It's important to find outlets for that tension, and regular physical exercise can be an easy solution.

As a Four, you're an excellent thinker! But you can be *so* good at it that you can get in your own way. You think and think and think about an issue and may end up overthinking and never moving forward with a decision. What can really drive your friends crazy is that your response to any question may be some form of "Let me think about it." It can be days or weeks—or even months or years—before that thinking process is complete!

As part of that quality, you pay special attention to timing, and if it doesn't quite feel right for something, you choose to wait before taking action. You can seem like an excellent procrastinator while family and friends wonder what in the world is going on in your head. Sometimes your emphasis on waiting for that perfect time results in your being absolutely right and hitting the jackpot! But overconcern about timing can also result in your missing opportunities as you focus on waiting for some absolute right moment.

Anna was a highly respected business coach who taught advanced trainings for professionals, but her workshops often didn't happen. It wasn't because she didn't have enough people interested—in fact, they were clamoring to take her courses. But Anna had a terrible time settling on a date for each session. She'd decide on one weekend but then would back off and remove it from her website schedule, wanting to think about it some more. Anna's students were continually frustrated and complaining that they couldn't rely on her to give them what they needed to complete their course, and eventually many went off to study with someone else who wasn't as good a teacher but who kept her schedule firm.

Some Fours live all in their heads. They're very analytical, interested only in theoretical concepts, and appear rather quiet and intellectual to others. But Fours can also be natural-born

poets and artists and choose creative lives. In addition, they're very idealistic and aware of all the suffering in the world; because of this, many Fours do philanthropic work or donate their time in their drive to change the world for the better.

Being out in nature is especially nurturing for your energy if you're a Four. You need to be physically active, but you may prefer a long, wandering hike over a short, focused run; or you will want to change it up with different kinds of workouts rather than go to the gym and use the same machines each day.

Careers

To determine the types of careers that align with your inner design, we need to consider the influence of both your first and third numbers, so be sure to read the description of your calling in Chapter 5 as well.

Fours are sometimes called "lane drifters." Imagine someone on the highway, driving in the left-hand lane, then the right, then the middle. . . . The pattern of changeability is the cause, and it appears throughout a Four's life. For example, they may live many different places or have a variety of jobs over the course of their lives. If this happens, it's often due to circumstances, not their deliberate choice, and certainly not a mistake; it's very much in alignment with that gentle wind nature that keeps blowing with the breeze!

You can thrive in structured kinds of organizations, bureaucracies like the government or corporations, changing the system from the inside. With your flexible spirit, you can get along with a wide variety of personality types, and you're usually described by everyone as very easy to work with. You could do well in management, not only because of your people skills but also due to your ability to navigate change so easily.

Your idealism may have you working for a nonprofit organization; or if you find success as an entrepreneur, it may well be that any business you start is either one intended to benefit humankind, or else you'll donate a percentage of the profits to charity.

Any job done out in nature could make you happy, such as work as an ecologist or nature photographer. With your flair for systems and design, you'd do well in careers such as analyst, landscape architect, or urban planner. Other fields could include woodworking or construction; and because of the influence of the theme of wind, I find that many airline pilots are Fours!

You'll be an excellent mentor in any field, and you could be an especially talented coach or consultant because you can easily see the direction your client needs to go but will never push or force them to change. Instead, you'll guide them as if with a gentle hand on their back, easing them in the right direction without ever seeming to push.

First Number: Five
Center

If you're a Five, you are a force of nature! Powerful, resilient, endlessly caring, and resourceful, you can show up as a strong support for others in life. In nature, this energy is associated with the earth—the solid ground beneath our feet and our source of nourishment—and that's definitely the essence of who you are. People just seem to sense that you're the best possible person to help them, and they naturally gravitate to you, so much so that it can sometimes feel as if you're the center of everyone's universe. It can certainly be gratifying to be called on so frequently, but at times it can feel like people are always asking you to do things for them but not showing adequate appreciation or thinking to return the favor.

Even so, you're always drawn to helping others, particularly due to your inherent good sense and skillful approach. You're a natural problem solver, and it's easy for you to spot errors in a system or see that others are going about something in the wrong way. But this characteristic can result in a bit of a know-it-all attitude because, frankly, you've rarely met anyone who has a better grasp of things than you do! When you can see that a plan is faulty, you'll want to speak up so that you can be sure things are well taken care of, and it will be hard to resist taking charge so that the work can get done more efficiently and successfully. But as a result, you may be perceived as demanding or controlling, although your intention is never to try to take over or dominate. You truly just want to help.

Need for Connection

You can be generous to a fault and will probably struggle with guilt if you ever have to say no to a request for help. Even though you've devoted the better part of your day—or week—to helping someone, you'll probably end up worrying that you didn't do enough and will check back again to see if there's anything else they need. Yet while you may be overly responsible and put everyone else ahead of yourself, at the same time, you can also feel taken advantage of or sense that people just take what you do for granted.

Fives can sometimes be judged as self-centered or demanding, but this is often the result of being misunderstood. They want to feel fully connected, and how is that possible without giving each other time and attention? So they'll tend to expect that people will spend quality time *and* a significant quantity of time with them in order to really focus on them, but they're also very willing to give others that kind of attention as well.

While you have a powerful need for connection as a Five, you disdain superficial relationships, small talk, or shallow social interactions. Instead, you have a lifelong, nearly insatiable need for deep bonds, to have a circle of friends who really "get" you, with whom you can have a certain level of conversation, and who recognize your abilities. You can also feel a frustration throughout life both personally and professionally that others are never fully aware of your efforts or how essential your work was in making an outcome successful. In fact, you may tend to feel vastly underappreciated in nearly every situation, and sometimes this is a valid conclusion. You also play a part in this because you're so focused on making sure everything works out successfully for everyone that you can end up angry at yourself for not claiming the credit you deserve.

The Influence of Resentment

Linda, a Five, volunteered to be in charge of organizing a big family reunion in her home. This was to be a very important event for a group of about 35 relatives, many of whom hadn't seen each other in years. She planned for months in advance, helped people coming in from out of town with travel arrangements, coordinated airport pickups, let several family members stay in her home, and used her connections to get discounted hotel rates for the overflow. She made sure to find out about any dietary restrictions for everyone attending and tracked down old family recipes so that there would be a wonderful nostalgic meal for everyone to enjoy. (Fives love to feed people.)

She decorated the house inside and out and prepared a special PowerPoint presentation full of images from her family photo albums as entertainment for the evening. Her two sisters who lived locally offered to bring food so that she didn't have to work so hard, and she assigned each of them a specific dish to contribute so there wouldn't be any overlap or missing items.

Finally the big day came, and Linda was up at 5:00 A.M. to start cooking and finishing the preparations. As people began to arrive, she brought out homemade hors d'oeuvres, making sure everyone felt welcome and comfortable. But the sisters who'd promised to contribute food were late; it also turned out that they hadn't prepared what she'd asked them to, but had stopped at Costco on the way over and bought chips, dip, and boxed salads.

When it came time for the big meal, everyone gobbled it up and raved about how delicious everything was; but to Linda, no one really seemed to recognize how she'd cooked everything

from scratch, as well as all the trouble she'd gone to reviving the old family recipes. After dinner, most of the group settled by the TV to watch the game, and only a handful dutifully viewed her PowerPoint show. Some tried to help her clean up, but she soon told them not to bother. She realized she was just going to have to unload the dishwasher and do it all over again because they just weren't doing it right.

In the end, Linda was left fuming, feeling deeply unappreciated despite the effusive thank-yous, and resentful about the lack of support. In fact, her party was the talk of the family for years to come, but as for many Fives, that wasn't enough. She felt her relatives didn't fully recognize all she'd done.

Family and Relationships

Family can be a big issue throughout life for Fives, especially in their relationships with their mothers. Some experience a kind of role reversal in childhood, where they had to be the parent even when they were quite young. Others had it even worse, being raised by an emotionally disturbed or even abusive mother. Some Fives leave home at an early age because the family dynamics are so dysfunctional; in certain cases, it's only because of their tremendous personal strength that they're able to survive childhood emotionally intact. But even so, as adults, Fives may be called upon to deal with the family's needs and problems, sometimes even to the point of moving back home. This can make them feel stuck and resentful—especially if it's a situation where they weren't well supported emotionally as children—and there they are, giving, giving, and giving, when they never had received much in the first place.

Aside from family, relationships of all kinds are a priority in your life, and you'll try at all costs to keep a friendship intact. Grace, a Five, taught workshops about developing intuition. She'd worked for ten years to create a structured training with thick handouts that really helped her students hone their skills; people were getting phenomenal results. A friend organized a workshop for her and in return got to attend for free. This friend then turned around and published her class notes as a book, plagiarizing Grace's handouts and only slightly changing the names of her methods.

When Grace discovered this, she agonized for an entire year before deciding to just let it go. It was too painful for her to imagine losing the friendship, especially because this was a person who had obviously deeply recognized the power of her work, something that's so important to a Five!

Extremes

Some Fives experience extremes in life, and the pattern can be one of a difficult childhood followed by both highs and lows as an adult, great success followed by some level of hardship. They may even have financial problems intermittently throughout life. But the good news is that as they age, things get easier and they can become financially stable.

A Five's personality can range to extremes as well. These are usually not mild-mannered, easygoing types; their deep personal power can be expressed in correspondingly powerful emotions. I advise people to never make a Five angry because they can be blasted by hurricane-force winds in response! But a Five's love and support is every bit as strong, and anyone lucky enough to have a Five as a friend knows the enormous lifelong benefits of that relationship.

Some Fives are ambitious and driven to claim a place of high achievement in the world, and they can even behave unethically to attain it. But at the other end of the spectrum, it's almost as if some are afraid of their own power. They can be shy and insecure or keep their lives small almost as an attempt to suppress what feels dangerous to them.

Careers

To determine the types of careers that align with your inner design, we need to consider the influence of both your first and third numbers, so be sure to read the description of your calling in Chapter 5 as well.

You're an incredibly good student, catching on quickly to new subjects; and once you pick up a skill, you'll look for ways to put it to use. So no matter what kind of career you have, it's likely that you'll always be adding to your abilities and integrating that knowledge into your work soon after.

Even so, you may continue to struggle with issues of low self-confidence that can affect your success. As much as you may have a know-it-all personality, you can also flip into worrying that you don't know *enough*, or you may have had such a lack of support in childhood that you don't have the natural Five confidence you could have gotten if there'd been a healthy environment at that time. Some Fives also have high self-esteem and low integrity—for example, one woman started promoting herself as certified after only an introductory workshop in coaching rather than completing her full professional training.

Fives are often found in the fields of business, real estate, education, and law; but a large percentage of them are also in the helping professions, such as social work, nursing, or the healing arts. Yet no matter what they do, they're more likely than most to end up at the center of an organization or even be its founder. Even if they're part of a team, though, it will be very important to them to not be left out of anything, and again, this can be misunderstood by others as the Five trying to be in control. It's not that; it's their inherent need to be in the middle of the action—and that's actually where they belong!

First Number: Six
Father

Like the archetypal Father who's in charge of the family, you are designed to be a natural leader who makes sure things get done and done well. With your mental clarity, you're able to see both the big picture and the fine details in any situation, and you project into the future to anticipate anything that could go wrong and prevent it from happening. Your focus will be on the long view, on what's most important, and you even have the potential to be quite a visionary in terms of helping us see the ideal life we should all aspire to.

The theme for the Six nature is also understood as representing heaven, meaning our connection with the Divine. You'll feel drawn to living a sacred life, but not necessarily in terms of spirituality or religion. You will certainly feel called to do meaningful work and to live authentically. You may consider your time to be sacred and resist having to do things that are trivial or seem to be a waste of your valuable resources and energy.

As a Six, you have very high principles and excellent manners, and you'll be bothered by people who exhibit a lack of awareness of others. It may drive you crazy at the grocery store when someone obliviously blocks the aisle with their shopping cart or carries on a loud cell-phone conversation in public, disturbing everyone around them.

Need to Achieve

Many Sixes end up holding power in some way, but even if you don't achieve what's thought of as a position of authority, you *will* need to feel proud of your accomplishments and respected by others. And while at times everyone ponders what their true calling in life might be, you could feel compelled to discover and fulfill your authentic purpose in order for your existence to feel worthwhile.

You care very much about the quality of your work and will tend to be precise and painstaking with whatever you do. However, you can also struggle with perfectionism. Because of this, criticism from others is almost too much to bear, and you may interpret a comment as critical even if it wasn't intended to be.

This reminds me of what Claire, a student of mine, once shared with me about her friend Leslie, a Six. Leslie had been invited to be a keynote speaker at a major conference, which was a huge honor. Claire decided to attend the conference, too, to sit in the audience and give moral support.

Leslie worked extremely hard on her speech for weeks. When the big day came, she confidently sat on the podium with the two other speakers. The first one got up, gave a brilliant presentation, and received a standing ovation. But Claire noticed that he had covered many of the points that Leslie was about to make. Then the second presenter gave his speech, again to a huge response, but this man said almost everything else her friend was about to share! When Leslie spoke, it sounded as though she was just parroting what had already been said, although obviously she'd prepared her talk in advance. At the end of her speech, there was only feeble applause. For a Six, this was a nightmare—a public failure.

Claire leapt to her feet as the speakers came down from the stage, and started hurrying toward her friend to comfort her after this terrible turn of events. But as soon as Leslie got close enough to recognize the stricken expression on Claire's face, she turned on her heel, walked away, and didn't speak to her again for weeks. To this highly sensitive woman, the look on her friend's face was unbearable. It was like criticism to her because it felt like an acknowledgment that she'd done something wrong.

The Influence of Sensitivity

You're probably not *that* sensitive to criticism, but it may be true that you are in fact highly sensitive overall. For one thing, you're hyperaware of details. You may be the one who immediately spots the typo in the letter or notices that the curtains aren't the exact shade of blue that was ordered. If you do find something wrong with a project (and you will!), it will be difficult to hold back from bringing it to someone's attention. It's as if you can't feel comfortable in your own skin until things are as perfect as they can possibly be.

Your body is also sensitive to subtle energy. Whether you're conscious of it or not, you can be physically affected by the energy of the people and places around you. You may feel stressed in crowded places—your idea of a nightmare might be the mall during the Christmas shopping season! It can even be uncomfortable if someone stands too close to you or if a stranger rushes up to give you a tight hug on your first meeting. If you have a little time to get used to their energy, then you'll be fine, but in general you'll feel better with a little more space than most people need. However, this can give others the impression that you're cold or aloof, or worse, that you're conceited and holding back because you think you're better than they are. This is not the case; you're simply trying to get comfortable with what you're feeling.

It's so important to recognize that when you walk into a room, you soak in a thousand times more information than most people do. You can be bothered by the details your five senses pick up: a picture is half an inch crooked on the wall, there's a smudge on the window, and someone in the room is wearing strong perfume. But whether you're consciously aware of it or not, you'll also be affected by what your sixth sense tunes in to: the subtle energy that's present. For instance, if someone is radiating stress or upset, you may begin to feel physically uncomfortable. At the extreme, some Sixes are so sensitive that if they walk into an empty room where an argument happened days ago, they'll be affected by the residue of energy left by the intense emotions experienced in the space and can start to feel unwell.

It can be overwhelming at times to have this level of sensitivity; in fact, your energy can hover half in and half out of your body because it's too much to come fully in and feel everything

there is to feel. Other issues can be a struggle with anxiety, the need for a lot of time alone and away from the intensity of the world and the people in it, or a tendency toward allergies or environmental sensitivities. Sixes often have a highly developed sense of smell and can notice an offensive odor when no one else in the room detects anything.

Because of your sensitivity to both the visible and invisible in the world, you may need things just so in order to feel comfortable, and thus can be perceived by others as nitpicky or controlling. But this just stems from your attempts to manage your experience in life, which too easily sends you into system overload.

Please keep in mind that this sensitivity is actually a powerful gift. Because you're so aware of nuances and subtleties, whatever you produce is perfectly done. You are also exquisitely attuned to other people's energy and thus have the potential to become an amazing teacher, advisor, or healer because you can sense which slight shift is the perfect one to produce change. I can't exaggerate what a positive and powerful presence you can be once you learn to manage your boundaries and not absorb everyone's energy.

As a Six, you may very well need help to find your power within this sensitivity. Otherwise, you'll always be caught up in the struggle to cope with what feels like a constant energetic assault from the world around you. Our culture doesn't acknowledge the reality of this kind of experience, and therefore many Sixes blame themselves, thinking something is terribly wrong with them. Getting some training in breath work or energy work is often a life-changing experience.

Most Sixes deal with a constant undercurrent of anxiety and because of this need a predictable rhythm in life. They will place importance on being on time, will notice if someone is late, and will feel upset if *they* arrive late themselves. They will want to know as many details as possible in advance about an event so that they can prepare themselves, and some become quite rigid in their daily routines—for example, preferring to have the same meals at the same times of day because it's calming to always know what to expect. Sixes do not need *more* stimulation!

Air of Authority

Father takes charge, and he doesn't like to see his decisions questioned or his authority challenged. When Father says, "Get in the car, kids," the kids know they're supposed to drop everything and get in the car. They don't whine, "*Why* do we have to get in the car?" It's Mother's job to sweetly explain why we're all getting in the car and add, "Be sure to take your jacket, and did you remember to go to the bathroom?" Father just expects to be obeyed without any fuss. So Sixes naturally project the energy of authority, and they don't like to be argued with. There's a joke that Sixes always think they're right—and they are! It *is* usually true that because you so clearly see all the different aspects of the situation, your view is accurate.

In our culture, it's easier for men to be Sixes than it is for women because the power they naturally project is more socially acceptable. We all read and react to each other's energy, and when we feel the air of authority around a male Six, it feels appropriate because we've been socialized to expect men to carry themselves that way. But sometimes women who are Sixes report that when they walk into a room, before they even get a chance to say or do anything, they can feel people thinking, *Who does she think she is?*

If you're a female Six, being aware that others can feel intimidated by you or react as if you're putting on airs will let you compensate for that possibility early in the relationship. One way you can do this is to be very warm and gracious from the moment you meet someone and approach *them* rather than wait for the other person to reach out.

Most Sixes are gracious and accommodating, but some hold the energy of authority so strongly that they carry a sense of entitlement. One unemployed Six believed he shouldn't have to interview for jobs because it was beneath his dignity—companies should just recognize his worth and offer him a position! One woman said that her Six husband never lifted a finger around the house despite the fact that they both worked full-time. And throughout five moves during their 15-year marriage, he always managed to be out of town at the time of the move, so she ended up having to take care of everything herself.

Dealing with Loss

A common emotional pattern for Sixes can be a sense of regret or fear of loss or lack. It may be that you hold on to grief, finding it difficult to let go and move on. It can even show up in minor ways, such as always turning to look backward, longing for the "good old days." Or it can be that even though your current situation is painful, you're afraid of change because what if you let go of this and there's nothing there to replace it?

If you never come to accept loss, you can't emerge into the next stage beyond grief, which is the discovery of what you gained through that experience and how you've been enriched by it. There's a beautiful resolve that comes after that realization, and a higher level of awareness, if you can let go and trust the process. When you learn to navigate life in this way, you are in your power.

Careers

To determine the types of careers that align with your inner design, we need to consider the influence of both your first and third numbers, so be sure to read the description of your calling in Chapter 5 as well.

With your natural ability to hold authority, you can succeed in any career where you're the one in charge. You can be a leader in business and politics, even quite a visionary in whatever field you choose. You'll also do well in any career that requires exquisite attention to detail, such as surgeon, acupuncturist, or accountant. And because of your strong sense of the sacred, spiritual work can be very fulfilling. Many clergy members, spiritual teachers, and counselors are Sixes.

First Number: Seven
Artist

Charming, gracious, and very aware of what's going on around you, you have a flair for creating beauty wherever you go. It may be that you create works of art, but it can just as easily be that you dress with style, design a lovely home environment, or give other people beautiful experiences because you're an excellent communicator and make anyone feel at ease and welcome.

Because you have such a sensitivity to nuances, subtleties, and details, if you're not an actual artist, you're *like* the Artist in whatever you do. You always strive to refine things, to make them as perfect and beautiful as they can possibly be. To that end, a Seven who's a highly respected therapist commented that she doesn't see her work as being about helping people at all: "It's an art form."

You are very good at reading others and can be almost chameleonlike in your ability to shift your energy to match another person's so that they feel comfortable and accepted. This is a lovely quality, but the problem is that if you go through each day constantly trying to vibrate at everyone else's frequency, when do you get to be yourself? You may need time alone at the end of each day to recover from all the hard work you've been doing invisibly to accommodate everyone around you. You need a chance to just be yourself.

Getting It Right

Sevens can be perfectionistic and overanalytical in many aspects of their lives, always worried about being good enough, doing something well enough, anxious about getting every detail right. They can even be tentative about committing to a job or a person, for instance, for fear there could be something even more perfect around the next corner. Or they may commit and then back off, wanting more time to think things through. One woman's Seven boyfriend proposed to her, and then two weeks

later told her he needed to go away to give himself time to think, to be really sure this was the right relationship for him! He was so sensitive, he actually couldn't even stay in the same city with her because her energy felt too close for him to be able to think clearly. After two months, he returned, saying he was now sure she was the one for him, but for the rest of their marriage she carried the hurt of feeling that if he really loved her, he would have been sure from the start.

An artist is concerned with how something looks, and for Sevens, that's true in many ways. It's interesting that the nature image for the Seven is of the surface of a lake—the smooth sheen that appears on a perfectly calm lake, not a ripple in sight. Some Sevens are very concerned with image and how things appear on the surface. If there's trouble in their lives, they may act as if everything's just fine; they can go into denial more easily than other people, trying to keep the surface of that lake looking perfect. They hope that if everyone can just agree that everything is pretty, then it will be—so please, let's just not talk about it. They can do this in their own minds as well, not admitting to themselves that they have a problem, sometimes remaining in denial for years, hoping that somehow if they pretend things are fine, they will be.

Like Sixes, many Sevens can also physically sense when the energy around them is "off," whether it's the energy of the room they've just entered or of the people standing in it. But this is often not obvious to the outside observer because the Seven can maintain such poise. It's only if things start to go wrong in ways the Seven can't control that the ripples appear on the lake!

In those cases, the Seven's charm can start to seem a little forced; they can appear a little too bright and cheery for the situation at hand, and people can think they're insincere or even lying. This isn't the case at all—they're just doing the best they can to make things seem okay.

The Perfect Hostess and the Princess

I call the Seven the Artist because their attention always goes to making things beautiful. But this isn't just in terms of appearances; they also strive to create beautiful *experiences* for others, which is why I also describe the Seven as the Perfect Hostess. They'll do everything they can to make people happy and give them the very best experience possible—whether that's just a 30-second conversation in an elevator or a 30-year relationship. This is a truly lovely quality, but taken too far, it can make them too much of a pleaser, and cause other challenges.

If you imagine the Perfect Hostess inviting 10 people to a dinner party but 13 show up, well, what does she do? She rushes off to the kitchen, where she rearranges the food and brings out 13 full plates. But then she sits down to an empty place setting herself, waving her hand and declaring that she's had a late lunch so she'll just sip her wine and enjoy their company—even though she's actually famished. There's a potential pattern of behavior in a Seven's nature that centers around deprivation. They'll deprive themselves in an attempt to make things as perfect as possible for everyone else.

This natural graciousness and artistic flair brings us to another nickname for the Seven nature: Princess. (This isn't meant as a derogatory term; it's representative of their charming nature.) The stereotypical Princess is a lovely girl whose life centers around glamorous parties and who lives in a beautiful palace—but she's not the one scrubbing the floors! So in some ways, the Seven, while always kind and conscientious, is a free spirit who won't seek out heavy responsibility in life.

Cynthia, a Seven who was a real-estate agent, struggled to earn enough—not because she wasn't experienced and knowledgeable, but because she wasn't willing to make the effort to sell herself to potential clients or go the extra mile to help out someone who might become a client in the future. She just didn't want to work that hard.

Carrying Responsibility

The most unfortunate part of this equation is that if responsibility *is* given to Sevens, they can take it far too seriously and let it weigh very heavily on their shoulders. There's a dual nature here: The Princess just wants a beautiful life, but if that isn't possible, she seems to transform herself into Cinderella instead, going to extremes in depriving herself to try to make things lovely again.

The most dramatic example of this in my work was Kathleen, a woman who was caring for and financially supporting her elderly parents, both in their 90s, so they could stay in the family home where they'd lived for the past 60 years. She had two brothers, neither of whom was contributing. They wanted to move their parents to a retirement home and sell the house, using the profits to pay for the facility. But Kathleen knew it would be traumatic for her parents to be taken from their home; in fact, with her sensitivity, it was physically painful for her to imagine it. So she paid for all their needs. She'd work all day and then cook them a homemade dinner, clean their house, and prepare breakfast and lunch for the next day. She had no time for herself, but it gave her joy to know that her parents could stay in the home they loved.

This all worked fine until Kathleen lost her job and couldn't find another. She asked her brothers to chip in, but they insisted on sticking to their plan, which she just couldn't agree to. She couldn't tell her parents what had happened. She knew they'd be upset and worried about her and would give up their home and probably die from the stress of the move. So Kathleen drained her savings to continue taking care of them, eventually losing her condo, going bankrupt, and living in her car rather than endure the pain of making her parents move.

As a Seven, it's vitally important for you to honor your conscientious nature but be able to set boundaries and not deprive yourself by trying to make things perfect. The ideal Princess doesn't order people around or force them to do her bidding, nor does she have to be afraid to ask for what she wants—or worse, do without entirely. She's just naturally taken care of. When you're in balance, you can see that you're perfect and enough just as you are, and that's when life brings you new options you weren't able to receive before.

Perfectionism Run Wild

A Seven loves to live in a beautiful home, and some also struggle with allergies and environmental sensitivities, so they're careful to keep their spaces extremely clean. But in some cases it's possible for the Seven nature to click into the exact opposite—they are the most likely of all the personality types to become hoarders. It's not because they don't care or that they're messy people. Rather, there are two common reasons why Sevens can transform their homes from palaces into hovels: One is that they have the potential to suffer from some degree of obsessive-compulsive disorder, which can be expressed as perfectionism run wild. They can be so anxious about doing things right that they don't do them at all. They may not throw out any papers for fear of discarding something they might need; or worst case, in their delusion, they can't put a container of spoiled food into the garbage because a speck might fall on the floor and contaminate the house.

The second reason a Seven can become a hoarder is also due to anxiety. They feel unsafe and build clutter as a buffer against the world, much as someone would gain weight. But one solution can ease both problems, and that's dealing with the high level of sensitivity that's the cause of the anxiety. Sevens can benefit greatly from training in meditation or energy work because it helps them manage their sensitivity and establish better energetic boundaries. Even just acknowledging how affected they are by subtle energy can be transformational.

Careers

To determine the types of careers that align with your inner design, we need to consider the influence of both your first and third numbers, so be sure to read the description of your calling in Chapter 5 as well.

You can excel in communications, so careers in writing, public speaking, or the media are options. Because of your awareness of beauty, you could find success as an interior designer, fashion designer, florist, jewelry maker, fine artist, or graphic designer.

Your precise attention to detail also serves you well in the field of finance, such as accounting or banking; in research; or in foreign-language translation. And the Perfect Hostess mentality can benefit you professionally as an event or wedding planner or hotel concierge. But your free-spirited Artist nature doesn't like to be tied down to a job, so you can be attracted to freelance work that allows you that freedom.

First Number: Eight
Transformer

In nature, the image for an Eight is the mountain, which is immovable. You can lean on a mountain, and as an Eight, you hold that kind of energy: hardworking, reliable, steadfast, and with enormous personal strength. You're also the most generous of all the types! You naturally want to support others, and your work for them can be on a grand scale. You'll step up to meet the needs of your family members, your friends, friends of your friends, and the community at large, no matter how hard the work or great the responsibility. You may love to bring large groups together for work or activities, especially if it benefits others. Although you may not be the social type, and you do need your solitude, your energy will always turn toward your connections or your tribe in some way. Home as well as family is important to you. Many Eights own more than one property; some even rent out homes at below-market rates so that people in need have housing.

As much as Eights are generous and giving, a common difficulty is a lack of receptivity, which can be a major challenge in life on many levels. The process of healthy giving is actually a two-way street. There's the act of giving and then there's the act of opening your arms to receive. Frequently Eights don't recognize that they lack the ability to soften and allow things to come to them, or for others to help and support them; if they don't work on this, over time it can build into stagnation in their lives.

Your mountain nature gives you enormous stamina and resilience, so you bounce back better than anyone else. And it's a good thing you do, because you take on challenges that would flatten someone else. As an Eight, you're called the Transformer because you use hard work for powerful personal growth on a very deep level.

Going Within

In the mountain, there is a cave, and that cave is where the transformation happens. You can picture the adept going far into the cavern to meditate and do deep inner work, which is the alchemical process of becoming a sage. You carry that personal cave within you as you embrace your life struggles, transforming them into profound strength and power mentally, emotionally, and spiritually.

But to the rest of the world, it may appear as though you just create struggle for yourself. Time and time again you choose what looks like the hard way in life. Friends and family scratch their heads as they watch, saying, "You want to do *what* now? Wouldn't it be a lot easier just to do this instead?" It's not a mistake in judgment for you to choose the more difficult path, though, because it's through the struggle that you learn the most. You may sign up for some demanding and lengthy course of study, tackle a job that most others just give up on, or stick with a relationship that

seems doomed because of all the problems involved. You do it because in the end, you benefit greatly from all you've learned; you've grown so much because of your hard work. Of course, this isn't always a conscious choice on your part, and life can hand you opportunities that you simply have to work through. These are patterns of nature, and just as an oak tree grows acorns, you have an inherent tendency to take on or be given some serious work.

The Influence of Deep Thought

A cave can also be used to retreat from the world for the purpose of contemplation. As an Eight, you'll tend to be a deep thinker, perhaps with an interest in philosophy or personal growth, and you'll need to think through decisions slowly and carefully. You'll want to retreat on a regular basis to de-stress and be alone with your thoughts, which may be in your own "cave" in the house (such as a basement getaway or a den), or it can mean a need to retreat before you can move forward. If you and your partner are arguing, it's best for them *not* to follow you around the house, saying, "We've got to resolve this *now!*" Instead, they should back off and give you some space to ponder the situation. Then you'll be able to emerge and work things out.

Another way to understand the cave is that this is where the treasure is, and the treasure is knowledge. You love to study and learn and may have an extensive library in your home, take seminars, or do self-development work. And because you're so nurturing, you'll want to teach people what you've learned or in some way use all your accumulated wisdom to help them discover their own hidden treasure and become the best they can be.

Accumulating treasure in the cave can mean more than just knowledge, however. Eights can be quite good at accumulating wealth or partnering with someone who does well financially. But accumulation can also be expressed as clutter, so Eights will need to take care not to let too much stuff build up around them or else have plenty of storage!

Despite the fact that your attention is always so oriented toward other people, you're not a chatterbox. You tend to be quiet and people may complain that you're hard to get to know, or your partner can feel cut off because you don't talk about what's going on inside. That's another influence of that inner cave, which is where part of you always tends to hang out.

No one can move a mountain, and you can indeed be immovable in your opinions or just stubborn overall. Part of the reason that you're not easily swayed is due to your solid thinking skills. It's been your experience that other people don't tend to think things through very well, so why should you be inclined to doubt your own conclusions? Sometimes, however, you can be like a dog with a bone. You just won't let an issue go, and people may as well give in if they're in that kind of tug-of-war with you!

Fairness and Justice

You usually appear calm and quiet and aren't easily provoked, but there are times the mountain can turn into a volcano! Your anger can be powerful and righteous, and it often centers around issues of unfairness or injustice, which are personal hot buttons for you. If you see someone being treated unfairly, you'll be the first to step up to protect them; and if you feel someone has done something unjust to you, they'll hear about it.

Melanie, an Eight, discovered a hairdresser in her town who did beautiful work and offered 10 percent off a haircut if anyone referred a friend. So she referred three friends who were so happy that they started referring *their* friends. Melanie got three discounts, but then demanded that the hairdresser also give her 10 percent off for each of her friends' friends who came in. She was so outraged when she was turned down that she stopped using the stylist's services, even though this person was the only one in town who'd done a good job on her hair.

Youngest Son

Another way the Eight is pictured is as the Youngest Son in a family. This doesn't mean you'll literally be the youngest child; it's that you carry that energy in your personality. The Youngest Son is in a peculiar position within the family because in being around the older family members, he soaks in all of their knowledge, so he's really very wise—but he's also still just a little boy. This can be expressed in an Eight's nature as naïveté, a lack of self-confidence, or at times feeling awkward and uncomfortable around others. You can visualize a little boy at a grown-up party, wandering around among all the adults, not knowing how to act or what's expected of him, and feeling very out of place and unsure of himself. This may be a recurring pattern of experience for Eights.

In situations where an Eight feels stressed, they may react childishly, behave in emotionally immature ways, or make impulsive decisions based purely on their feelings. Terence was a chiropractor whose patients adored him—and rightly so, because he was the typical warm and generous Eight personality. But Terence was awful at running his business. He was disorganized, couldn't keep an assistant for more than a few months, and was late paying his bills and doing his paperwork. Finally the state board started an investigation. Terence became so upset that one day, he just locked the door of his office and walked away. He immediately took a job as an airport shuttle driver, still helping people but in a much less demanding way.

Careers

To determine the types of careers that align with your inner design, we need to consider the influence of both your first and third numbers, so be sure to read the description of your calling in Chapter 5 as well.

Because you care so much about fairness and justice, we might find you in the fields of law, mediation, social services, or human rights, doing pro bono work or fighting for the underdog in some way. The core of your nature is about facilitating transformation, so you can also be happy working in education, personal development, or health care.

Eights can be very successful in business, and they'll always treat their staff or employees like family, going out of their way to help in sometimes incredibly generous ways. Home and the land are important, so you find Eights in real estate—especially appraisal, property management, or development—or in the hospitality industry. And because the Eight also has a theme of nurturing and nourishment, careers in nutrition, food services, or caregiving are also options. Many Eights are deeply spiritual and talk about how they long to create a retreat center in a remote location on a large piece of land where people can come to do inner work.

But no matter what profession you end up in, if you do find big success, you tend not to sit back, put up your feet, and enjoy the rewards. Instead, you can become even more single-minded and work even harder. It's important to learn to balance hard work with time to enjoy the fruits of all your labor.

First Number: Nine
Lover

The strongest theme running through the nature of a Nine is that of the heart. Incredibly warm and openhearted, these people are here to spread love, and their attention will always be drawn to giving affection to everyone they meet. Because they have a natural desire to connect with others, most (not all) Nines have an easy time making friends. They tend to have a sparkle about them, and an easy charm. Some are blatantly flirtatious—but it's not about a sexual come-on. They'll flirt with men, women, babies, and dogs walking down the street. It's all about opportunities to exchange little sparks of love from heart to heart!

As a Nine, you're great at bringing a lighthearted vibe to any interaction and you can always crack a joke to bring everyone's spirits up. Vivacious and charming, you have an inherent exuberance and may even talk quickly and wave your hands around as you speak. Because of this vibrant nature, you're good at getting other people excited about something, making them feel inspired and uplifted. For you, life is about passion and doing the things that light you up, especially if that can be with people you love.

Flickering Flame

In nature, the Nine relates to fire, and one way to understand your personality is that of a joyfully flickering flame. Because of this, at times you can find other people's attitudes a bit heavy and wonder why they can't just lighten up. You're a free spirit and love to have fun—in fact, you don't think something's worth doing unless it's fun. A quick learner and highly creative, you have a very active mind and can hardly find enough time to do everything you want to do. Change and variety are important to you, and like fire looking for new things to burn, you constantly seek out new experiences. Your worst fear is being bored, but that's hardly a possibility!

Thank goodness you're quite good at multitasking because you'll always have many balls in the air. You can have trouble settling in to pay attention to one thing for any length of time and actually do best if you can work on different projects for short bursts, changing your focus frequently. Yet even then, you'll have trouble completing tasks and need to take care that you don't become scattered. You'll be working on 23 different priorities but suddenly see something sparkly out of the corner of your eye and think, *Oh, <u>that</u> looks like fun!* and then everything falls into chaos.

Being a Nine can mean that you end up in the spotlight in some way. Nines are said to be natural performers who easily draw people's attention. It may just be that you light up a room the minute you walk in or that you have a talent for performing or public speaking. Nines just tend to get noticed more easily than other people do, and it can be important to them to feel special in that way. At the extreme, some are quite vain and self-centered, always wanting the conversation to focus on *them* and how fabulous they are. A Nine once confirmed this in one of my workshops, saying, "Oh, yes, I'm all that and then some!"

The Vulnerable Heart

Some Nines are not like the previous description at all. Instead they're shy and quiet and don't like to have attention focused on them. This brings us to some challenges that you as a Nine might experience in different ways. You have a very open heart, but an open heart is also a vulnerable one. Nines tend to wear their hearts on their sleeves; if someone is unkind or rejects them, it can be far more painful than it would be for others. Some Nines find that possibility so frightening that they avoid any chance of someone not liking them. A Nine who was a consultant had trouble getting work—not because she wasn't brilliant at her job, but because she had to schmooze with potential clients in order to get hired. She was so terrified of rejection that she couldn't bring herself to network or socialize.

Nines are naturally cheerful and sociable people, yet there's often a very solitary place inside where they really live. They may have lots of friends but not many close ones, or their relationships don't last for long. They'll always yearn to have people in their lives who find them truly special. The background fear is that they may not really be lovable. This is why the infatuation stage in a romance is usually their favorite part, because the thrill of being the center of someone's universe makes them feel totally lovable.

As a Nine, your emotions will always be close to the surface and tears can easily come—not just when you're sad, but anytime you feel a surge of love for someone. (For instance, a parent who's a Nine will invariably cry when they talk about their children.)

But your feelings can also easily be touched off by the emotions of others. A student in a recent workshop called himself a "contact crier" because whenever anyone else cried, he'd immediately burst into tears.

The Influence of Anxiety

Some Nines are excitable, love stimulation, and seek intense experiences—even to the point of creating big drama in their lives. But if this doesn't sound like you, it may be that your experience is a tendency toward anxiety instead of drama. The Nine energy is like a hummingbird's: a very high vibration that's like being high-strung or nervous. It can be a revelation to discover what contributes to these feelings: you're an empath.

Let me explain what that means. Chinese medicine teaches that our consciousness does not reside in our brains; instead, it lives in our hearts. So as a Nine with such an open heart, you also have a very open consciousness, which is lovely—but it also means that you can be affected by the thoughts and feelings of other people without being aware of it.

One of the reasons you may be a contact crier is that it's so easy for you to make an energetic connection with the consciousness of another person. They don't even have to be in the same room. For example, you may sense when a friend is about to contact you because they just come to mind—and then the text arrives or the phone rings.

But this empathic nature can cause problems as you're bombarded by the thoughts and emotions of other people, even if they're not in the same space. Christine, a Nine, had an exhibit of her artwork in a major gallery, and the local newspaper published an article about her. She didn't sleep well for the next few days as she was psychically impacted by the attention of hundreds of people reading the article, their thoughts directed to her, which jangled her nerves.

It can be empowering for you to become more aware of your energetic boundaries and realize that not every thought or feeling that passes through your awareness is actually yours! Once you begin to learn to identify what's yours and what isn't, you can develop your skills as an empath to gain a very high level of awareness, to the point that you could help others as an intuitive counselor or healer.

The Heart Protector

In Chinese medicine, there's an organ in the body called the Heart Protector, whose function is to act almost like a filter around the heart, to screen out what will be harmful and allow in what will be beneficial. Another term for it is the Gate of Intimacy. The gate swings wide open for someone you love and trust, but it should only open slightly for someone you don't know yet, gradually letting them farther in as you get to know them better.

With Nines, however, it's almost as if your heart is so huge that the filter of the Heart Protector gets stretched too thin and develops holes, or the gate can't fully close. The result in everyday experience can be that you may allow intimacy too soon. For instance, one woman moved in with a man after just two dates and had her heart broken because she trusted too quickly. In most cases if this happens, the Nine will feel terribly hurt for a while but recover and be able to return to their loving nature. But if their heart is shattered, one possible result is that they'll lose their joy and come across as flat or dispirited from that point forward.

Alternatively, the Nine may from then on only maintain the most superficial relationships, never again really letting anyone into their heart. Some performers are like this, only feeling happy and safe when they're up on a stage with an audience adoring them, but never having truly close relationships in their personal life. And sometimes we see those whose gate has frozen wide open. They continually get involved with people they should

never have let into their hearts and suffer time and time again as a result.

Yet another possible response to hurt is that the Gate of Intimacy will instead slam shut and lock. When this happens, the heart closes and hardens to others. Vera, age 70, was in this state when she came to me for a reading. She hobbled into the office, her body racked with arthritis, and painfully sat down in the chair across from me. Her mouth was creased and turned down, and frankly, she looked mean. So I was surprised when I read Vera's birth date, to discover that not only was she a Nine but that her entire life theme was about the heart.

As I started explaining what this meant, that her true spirit was about the joy of connecting heart to heart, Vera's face twisted into disgust. With each word out of my mouth, she scowled more and rolled her eyes as if I were a complete moron. I wasn't falsely trying to cheer her up since I was also discussing the challenges of having such an open heart, but she was treating me like I was spewing nonsense.

I finally had to stop the reading and tell her that I couldn't continue if she wasn't going to be able to listen with an open mind, at least at first. I offered to not charge her for the session and just stop so that I didn't waste any more of her time. When she said that she wanted to continue, I went ahead, thinking, *Well, this is a lost cause.*

After a few more minutes Vera suddenly spoke up, telling me the story of how two friends had horribly betrayed her 40 years earlier, using the phrase "shattered my heart." She said she hadn't been the same since. She'd decided that she'd never again allow anyone to hurt her in that way, and from that day forward had no close friendships or romance.

But as we talked over the course of the next hour, I watched her bloom like a rose. She said that I was right, that she desperately wanted love in her life and had been a warm and outgoing person before her traumatic experience. She'd felt cut off from life for so many years and didn't know how to find her way back. Now Vera felt that my words were reawakening something in her.

She had a neighbor who seemed really nice—maybe she should invite the woman over for tea. And she'd heard about a church where the services were uplifting—she thought she'd give it a try. She'd always wanted a dog. If she had one, she could take it for walks and meet other people that way, too. In that short space of time, Vera's heart began to soften and new possibilities for love poured in. I was in awe of how quickly the light can return.

Careers

To determine the types of careers that align with your inner design, we need to consider the influence of both your first and third numbers, so be sure to read the description of your calling in Chapter 5 as well.

Because you're so good at getting people excited about things, you can find success in sales, marketing, public relations, performing, or teaching, keeping your audience laughing as they learn. Your talent in communications can land you a job in the media, and your natural creativity also inclines you to work in the arts. Careers in travel can be a great fit because of all the people you get to meet and the exciting places you can visit. Whatever field you choose, it will have to be fun and full of variety to keep you engaged.

As you've seen, your first number reveals many layers of meaning about your temperament, belief patterns, strengths, challenges, and personal potential. But there's so much more to come that can help you move through life in alignment with your true spirit. In the next chapter, we'll look at aspects of your *inner* nature, whose origins can be traced back to your childhood self.

CHAPTER 4

YOUR EMOTIONAL SELF

Your second number reveals your inner nature, your emotional self. It relates to what Western psychologists might call your inner child, that part of you that emerges in response to your feelings and your emotional reactions to life. This idea stems from the fact that children respond purely out of their emotions; that's where they live until they mature. This is the part of your personality that only those who know you well really see, although it can shine through the cracks to others, giving them a sense about you that they can't quite put a finger on.

So while this number does carry wonderful qualities, what's most helpful to understand is that it shows the feelings and behavior you revert to under stress or when you're upset. And of course because you don't become a *better* version of yourself when you're stressed, this pattern is often expressed in more negative ways that can cause further problems. It can be valuable to learn to recognize when your stressed self is surfacing and discover how to not get so lost in those feelings. Just gaining the awareness of your particular pattern of reaction can revolutionize your life because it gives you the power to catch yourself before you get swept away. You can understand that your stressed self is trying to take over!

The terms for each number to follow describe the stressed version of who you are and the strength within that quality that can help you return to a balanced state. I want to remind you that we're looking only at your second number here; for instance, if your numbers are 2.9.7, you would read the section about Nine.

Second Number: One
Fear/Courage

If your second number is a One, the good news is that you have a deep inner source of strength and wisdom that you can always summon. Read the section in Chapter 3 about One as a first number to get a sense of the positive qualities of Ones and know that you carry that essence within you. But since this is your second number, it will express itself differently from the first number because you mainly go there under stress; that is, you're more likely to exhibit the negative qualities rather than positive ones.

Having a One here means you may become stubborn when things get tough, digging in your heels and refusing to compromise or turning into a steamroller and trying to exert your will on everyone else. Or it could be that you withdraw when you're upset, needing time alone and not wanting to talk.

You feel things more deeply than people realize, and when you're stressed, your feelings can be easily hurt. If this does happen, that hurt may go quite deep, last for a long time, and not be easily resolved—because in this situation, you'll tend to clam up and not be able to talk things out.

It's so important for you to acknowledge that you may too easily get caught up in your emotions. However, the solution isn't in trying to suppress or deny your feelings, but in knowing that you're totally in charge of how seriously you take them. If you can wisely allow your emotions but not get lost in them, you'll find that they soon pass, and you're still in balance. You'll no longer have to find your way back to shore after being swept out to sea.

Another way stress can impact you is by bringing up feelings of fear, and this may be what you base your decisions on rather than reasoning things through. It could be that the fear makes you freeze, feeling as though you can't move forward because every option leaves you paralyzed with dread about what could happen.

But when you look deep inside the One nature, you discover your source of power: your tremendous courage. It can be hard to imagine how to reach your courage when you're lost in fear, but you do have a stepping-stone: wisdom. In other words, even within your fear, you have a special ability to know the truth. It's by accessing your wisdom about the situation that you find your courage and are able to move through the fear. As you summon your wise self, you're empowered to see things for what they are, not what you're afraid they might be.

You don't take everything a frightened child tells you seriously, and your wise self has that attitude here. As with a child, give yourself reassurance and take some time to talk yourself through the situation. You'll start to discover that you let your fears get bigger than they needed to be. Remember how you've always been able to deal with difficulties in the past, even if you weren't sure at the time, and that what you learned from those experiences has soaked in to make you even stronger today. *Now* you have the courage to proceed!

Second Number: Two
Worry/Calm

If your second number is a Two, the good news is that your inner self is grounded, with a sense of safety that you can tap into as you need. Read the section in Chapter 3 about Two as a first number to get a sense of the positive qualities of Twos and know that you carry that essence within you. But since this is your second number, it will express itself differently from the first number because you mainly go there under stress; that is, you're more likely to exhibit the negative qualities rather than positive ones.

Under stress, it's easy for you to lose confidence, and you can become so caught up in worrying that you're no longer able to think very clearly. It's not uncommon to feel as though you have to turn to others for help. Even if you're normally the kind of person who can deal with anything, you may suddenly drop into feeling disempowered and unsure.

Sometimes it's that you give up your power in pressured situations, sacrificing your needs for someone else's or even behaving codependently, losing yourself in the other person. At other times, there's the possibility of switching into victim mode, feeling sorry for yourself, or even falling into resentment because it seems like no one's there for you. This attitude prevents you from taking charge of the situation, and you can get locked into a "poor me" frame of mind that could take you down a road of negative thinking.

One note: It's more challenging for a man to have a Two as a second number than it is for a woman. The qualities of this number represent the most yin and "feminine" characteristics. This does *not* mean that a man with the Two inner nature isn't masculine, though! What it does mean is that when he's upset, the loss of confidence or power he feels is more distressing for him than for a woman because it feels emasculating. In our culture, of course, men are supposed to be confident and powerful, and here he's feeling the opposite of that.

When a man has an inner Two, his behavior under stress doesn't always appear to be a loss of confidence or a victim mentality. Instead, what he exhibits may seem like anger, which is one of the few emotions that's deemed acceptable for men in our society. When a man with an inner Two is stressed and falls into that powerless place, he can blast others because that's the only emotional outlet he has, and also because he's mad at himself for feeling weak. It can be so helpful for people to understand why this happens so that they can avoid reacting in kind.

Whether you're a man or woman, recognizing when one of these patterns shows up can help you immediately click out of the behavior. To save yourself from getting lost in powerlessness, you can summon the part of your inner nature that's your greatest strength: the Divine Feminine, which the Chinese call Quan Yin, the Goddess of Compassion. What it means for you is that in any moment of stress, it will help to remember that there's always a soft yet grounded place inside yourself to come home to. You have a sense of safety and inner calm that you can rest in, knowing that life loves you and will take care of you if you just let it.

Second Number: Three
Anger/Action

If your second number is a Three, the good news is that your inner self has a vitality, a dynamic energy that's always available to give you a power surge. Read the section in Chapter 3 about Three as a first number to get a sense of the positive qualities of Threes and know that you carry that essence within you. But since this is your second number, it will express itself differently from the first number because you mainly go there under stress; that is, you're more likely to exhibit the negative qualities rather than positive ones.

In nature, the image for a Three is thunder, and that explosive quality can show up when you're stressed as frustration or anger! It will be essential for you to choose positive ways to blow off steam when you're upset so that you don't end up yelling at people you care about, stomping out of a staff meeting, or getting caught up in road rage on the highway. Go for a run, or in the theme of thunder, make noise—sing, bang pots and pans in the kitchen, or shout into a pillow!

This thunder can also make you react too quickly and angrily to something someone says. Without taking time to compose your reply, you can end up causing an argument or hurting their feelings. There's a sense of urgency and the potential to make impulsive decisions that you'll later regret because you didn't think things through. The enthusiasm of the Three nature can cause impatience, a desire to just run with an idea and not deal with the boring details!

This energy also creates an inner tension that can be expressed as compulsive behavior. During difficult times, you may work compulsively or exercise for hours to try to work off the stress.

This could even contribute to self-injuring behavior such as cutting or addiction, whether to computer games, drugs and alcohol, or something more minor. This tendency also creates the potential for moodiness, even depression, with that negativity turned in toward yourself.

Lastly, a Three's competitive nature can take over, and they may behave without integrity just so they can win, or they could try to dominate the situation and push people around. Under stress, they may resist owning up to a mistake, refusing to apologize for an obvious goof or blaming someone else.

The power of your hidden nature is Warrior energy, your dynamic drive and ability to easily take action. You can learn to notice the moment that feelings of frustration or anger start to rise in your system and choose to direct them to constructive instead of destructive actions. When you're going through a stressed period, go into Warrior mode and stay physically active to use up some of that powerful drive. Direct your energy to creating a plan of attack for the situation and then take action based on that plan. Focus your attention on doing something to create positive change—your benevolent Warrior fighting to make things better in the world.

Second Number: Four
Waver/Adapt

If your second number is a Four, the good news is that you have an inner sense of adaptability, a flexible nature that allows you to easily adjust to changing circumstances. Read the section in Chapter 3 about Four as a first number to get a sense of the positive qualities of Fours and know that you carry that essence within you. But since this is your second number, it will express itself differently from the first number because you mainly go there under stress; that is, you're more likely to exhibit the negative qualities rather than positive ones.

Under stress, you may feel frustrated, indecisive, or unsure. It will seem as though there are so many options all of a sudden, and the way to go simply isn't clear. You may make a decision, then waver and back off from it to try another direction. You'll be likely to overthink things, and that can leave you feeling flustered and full of self-doubt. On top of that, you can beat yourself up for not being able to move forward, and that negative self-judgment is toxic to your process.

The more complicated the situation is, the more likely it is that your mind will start to splinter among all of the different aspects, and you may think it's best to just wait to decide. But that can turn into procrastination, stalling, and getting lost in uncertainty and frustration. Alternatively, you may become impulsive and jump into a decision without taking the time to be sure of yourself.

Although it's a good idea to get advice from friends or colleagues, you may resist it because you'll even overthink their conclusions; and you may be skeptical, wondering if they can be objective or fully understand the situation. In addition, you can be too easily influenced by other opinions and end up even more confused and unsure. While you were about to go with your plan A, one friend says to choose plan B, and the other says plan C is definitely the only way to go. Now your head is spinning.

Another way the Four nature can affect you under stress is that frustration builds and builds until suddenly the grass looks a lot greener—over there! You can have an urge to get away from the situation; for example, whenever one affluent European client of mine was under pressure, she'd go to the airport and just take the next flight out.

Under prolonged difficulty, the Four nature can incline you toward depression. If that goes untreated, it may ultimately transform into apathy, a sense of giving up entirely. But it never needs to reach this point. Instead, from the first moment stress takes you to your Four self, you can own your adaptable nature instead of judge it or get lost in it. Your greatest strength is how you can ride the wind through life. With awareness, you can learn to keep that wavering nature in balance by bending but always coming back to center. One way to do this is to have a grounded friend to discuss things with, and another is to not judge yourself for your fluctuations. Choose one plan, go with it, see what happens, and adjust accordingly—but keep moving. You can be a master of change!

Second Number: Five
Absorb/Intensify

Here's where we reach an interesting fact: If your second number is Five, the other two numbers in your sequence are identical. If you look at the chart at the end of Chapter 2, you'll notice that whenever the second number is a Five, the numbers on either side of it are the same. Take a look—you'll see 1.5.1, 2.5.2, 3.5.3, 4.5.4, and so on.

The character of the Five here is like tofu, soaking up all the other flavors in a dish. When a Five is your second number, therefore, it pretty much ceases to be a Five and becomes whatever the other two numbers are. So if your numbers are 1.5.1, your second number actually becomes more like a One; and in order to learn what your hidden nature is, you'll read the section about Ones above. If you're a 2.5.2, that Five becomes more like a Two, and you would read the section about Twos above, and so forth.

There's one exception: If you're a 5.5.5, read the section about your special combination in Chapter 5.

Second Number: Six
Anxiety/Power

If your second number is a Six, the good news is that you're the one we want around in an emergency! This is when your inner strength as Father will show up to take charge. Read the section in Chapter 3 about Six as a first number to get a sense of the positive qualities of Sixes and know that you carry that essence

within you. But since this is your second number, it will express itself differently from the first number because you mainly go there under stress; that is, you're more likely to exhibit the negative qualities rather than positive ones.

You'll want to take control when things are going wrong and everyone's feeling pressured. This can be fine in many cases because the character of Six is one that gives you clarity and keeps you from getting swept up in the drama of the problem. However, this inner nature also inclines you to become uptight under stress, insisting that things be done your way and getting too caught up in little details.

The reason you may be so controlling is that you become anxious. You're worried that others won't do the right thing or won't do it well enough. Because of this, people can think you're being critical of every little thing, and this could create huge opportunities for relationship problems on top of the current issue that caused the stress in the first place!

But another big factor to be aware of is how highly *self*-critical you can be, far too hard on yourself and fearful of making mistakes. You'll also be overly sensitive to criticism from others and more likely to misinterpret an innocent comment. In challenging times, your sensitivity may go into overdrive as well, and you can be bothered by little things that are usually no big deal to you.

The positive expression of the inner Six is the dad who retains his cool while everyone around him is falling apart, and who has the mental clarity to know exactly the right thing to do. "Father knows best" is actually the theme here! If Father is emotionally in balance, he doesn't act like a tyrant, criticize people, or get lost in self-criticism. Instead, he stands in a position of power, calmly taking charge, keeping his eyes focused on the big picture.

So it's helpful in these cases to step back and take the long view. Choose your battles, try not to micromanage, remind yourself that it's not all up to you to fix . . . and remember to breathe! You'll tend to breathe too shallowly when stressed and that can keep you locked in hypervigilance. A few deep breaths in moments of stress can do wonders.

Learn to notice when those feelings of Six anxiety start to rise in your system so that you can consciously respond to them differently. Rather than fall into behavior that other people will perceive as "control and criticize" (even though that's not your intention), remind yourself that this feeling is anxiety. Often, simply being able to name it can keep you from identifying with the feeling and getting so caught up in it. Knowing it's natural for you to feel anxious under stress can help you let those feelings just surface and move on. Remembering that you are more than good enough to deal with any situation can help you breathe and step into your power.

Second Number: Seven
Denial/Pleasure

If your second number is a Seven, you're very attuned to the energy of others when you're stressed. You can maintain your poise and make people feel at ease no matter how difficult your own situation is. Read the section in Chapter 3 about Seven as a first number to get a sense of the positive qualities of Sevens and know that you carry that essence within you. But since this is your second number, it will express itself differently from the first number because you mainly go there under stress; that is, you're more likely to exhibit the negative qualities rather than positive ones.

When you're stressed, you'll tend to deny your own needs in an attempt to make things lovely for everyone else. An everyday example of this could come up if you're in a group of people trying to choose a restaurant for lunch. You'll likely be the one to say, "Oh, I don't mind where we go. What are *you* in the mood for?" when actually you are craving Thai food or detest the Mexican place someone suggests.

Under stress, there's an inner chameleon here who changes to accommodate whoever you're with. That can be a charming quality, allowing you to create an easy rapport with others, but it can

prevent you from being your authentic self, even with friends. You may not be able to relax and just be who you are, and that can limit the growth of any relationship.

I have a nickname for people who have a Seven as their second number: Hostess on the Titanic. If you remember the description for Sevens as the Perfect Hostess, this is the stressed version of that pattern. The ship is sinking, but you're walking around with a bright smile, saying, "Would you like another drink?" and "Let's have the band play one more song!" When stressed, you can try so hard to make it look like everything's all right that it starts to seem insincere. Everyone knows the ship is sinking! It's not that you're lying—you genuinely want to make things better. You desperately hope that if you act as if everything is lovely, it will be.

But in the bigger picture, this is a strong tendency toward denial, hoping that if you just don't talk about the elephant in the room, if you just pretend everything is fine, it will be. If your second number is Seven, you can even be in denial with yourself about how bad a problem has gotten, rather than doing something about the situation.

Under stress, you may also become anxious and perfectionistic, worried about not being good enough or so concerned about finances that you'll work too hard and deprive yourself of rest, or become stingy and try to live on a shoestring.

The Perfect Hostess creates beautiful parties and experiences to give others pleasure, but she doesn't exhaust herself cooking and cleaning to make things just so! People enjoy whatever she creates not because she worked so hard to pull it off, but rather because she has such a naturally lovely way about her and they simply adore being with her.

In times of stress, consciously come back to this moment and remember that who you are is perfect, that you are enough just as you are. In any relationship, you can know that just being yourself will bring pleasure to the other person, and you have no other responsibility in any interaction. In your work, it's likely that even if you put in only 50 percent of your usual effort, that's probably the same as someone else's 100 percent! You don't need to overwork because you're trying to make things perfect and as a result deprive yourself of time for rest or fun. When you can let go, know that you're good enough, and enjoy whatever life brings you, then there's no reason for denial or deprivation. When you can relax into yourself in this way, every moment becomes full of pleasure.

Second Number: Eight
Retreat/Strength

If your second number is an Eight, you have an inner mountain, a deep source of strength and knowledge that you can always lean on. Read the section in Chapter 3 about Eight as a first number to get a sense of the positive qualities of Eights and know that you carry that essence within you. But since this is your second number, it will express itself differently from the first number because you mainly go there under stress; that is, you're more likely to exhibit the negative qualities rather than positive ones.

When you're upset, you need to retreat to your cave. You may literally seek solitude in a room that has four walls and a door that you can close—and maybe lock! If you can get time alone, you can compose yourself, think things through, and emerge with a different attitude and new decisions. Or retreat can mean that you just need people to back off and stop pushing you. It's hard for you to make decisions under pressure. You need time to contemplate, and that can only be done if everyone gives you some space.

There can be communication difficulties when you're stressed. Imagine sitting in a cave and trying to communicate with the outer world. Whether you're shouting from inside the cave or someone is talking to you from the outside, words can get garbled and the message can be misunderstood. When you're going through a difficult time, misunderstandings are likely to happen,

and not necessarily just during conversations. You may sign the contract without noticing that unfortunate clause or misread instructions for how to put that toy together on Christmas Eve.

You can get very single-minded under stress, and like a dog with a bone, not be able to let go of the issue. People may say that you're stubborn, but you feel that if they had any principles, they'd agree with you. Another frequent symptom of this determination is that you'll work far too hard, as if on some level you believe that you can work your way out of the difficult situation. Or you may click into the deeply nurturing side of Eight and end up diligently helping others and not taking care of yourself.

One final way the mountain can affect your personality is that when you're upset, it can turn into a volcano. Anyone with an Eight as a second number has a powerful potential for anger when they're stressed, and if it comes, everyone should stand back!

Another image for the Eight is that of the Youngest Son in the family. A little child surrounded by more mature and experienced relatives can feel inadequate and unsure. So when you're upset, you may suddenly lose self-confidence and doubt your ability to figure things out, or even behave impulsively or in an emotionally immature way.

The thing about the Youngest Son is that he actually soaks up all the knowledge the rest of his family members have gained in their lives so far, so he's extremely wise and capable. What can help when you're stressed is to realize that you actually know everything you need in order to move through this time. Any worried feelings are just a sign of that inner child's lack of confidence, and you can reassure that part of yourself that everything is okay.

Allow yourself solitude in times of stress, knowing it's like medicine for you. Retreat to your cave or give yourself time to think things through, and you'll do fine with any challenge. Remember that you can summon the strength of your inner mountain whenever you need it.

Second Number: Nine
Drama/Joy

If your second number is a Nine, your inner nature is all about the heart. You have an inner warmth and passion at your center that radiates love. Read the section in Chapter 3 about Nine as a first number to get a sense of the positive qualities of Nines and know that you carry that essence within you. But since this is your second number, it will express itself differently from the first number because you mainly go there under stress; that is, you're more likely to exhibit the negative qualities rather than positive ones.

Having a Nine for your second number means that under stress, your emotions and anxiety can flare up and you get so swept away by your feelings that you react only from that frantic place. Of course whenever anyone is stressed, it's hard to think rationally, but you can get so lost in your feelings that your reasoning ability is seriously diminished. You may make decisions that you later regret; lash out at a friend; or "catastrophize" a situation in your mind, unable to imagine how you'll ever survive this terrible time. At the extreme, someone with a Nine here can cause big drama or have panic attacks.

As the emotions are stirred or anxiety takes over, your attention can become too scattered, and the potential for careless actions soars. Rather than try to describe various ways this could happen, let me share a classic story that illustrates it.

Virginia, a woman who'd been married four times, confided in me, "I always have someone waiting in the wings!" She was engaged to be married for the fifth time, but her fiancé suddenly broke up with her. This had never happened before—*she'd* always been the one to leave. Her inner Nine went into freak-out mode, and she decided that she couldn't bear to stay in her town anymore because there were just too many memories. In fact, she couldn't manage being a mother because she was so upset. She decided to send her daughters to live with their father for the summer, and she was going to move to Miami. She'd never actually been to Miami before, but she figured that she'd get there and everything would work out.

The day before she and her girls were scheduled to leave town, Virginia had to take her oldest daughter to one last soccer game at school. As she settled into a seat in the stands with the other parents, she struck up a conversation with one of the fathers sitting next to her . . . and three weeks later, they were married in Hawaii! The marriage lasted barely two years.

Granted, that's an extreme example of how your inner Nine can affect you; usually the results are much less dramatic. But it is true that under stress you can go into overwhelm and want to get away from everyone and everything. This is part of what Virginia was feeling. And in fact, giving yourself a break really can help, but only a temporary respite is needed. If it goes on too long, it actually has a detrimental effect. Taking a vacation would have been a better solution for Virginia, but in her dramatic frame of mind, it wouldn't have seemed like enough.

In Chinese medicine, the heart is said to be the source of joy in the body. The energy of your heart goes out during the day to touch other hearts and exchange joy, and then it returns to your body at night to settle and calm itself, to rest while you sleep. When your second number is Nine, under stress, your heart is agitated and can lose its ability to maintain this healthy rhythm. Instead, it may choose to isolate itself by day, and/or stay too active at night, causing insomnia.

In difficult times, there are ways you can restore your equilibrium. First, use physical movement to burn off some of the agitated energy—even literally jumping up and down for a few minutes can make a difference! Second, it can ground you to be with people you love, to talk through your problems, or to escape the difficulties with some laughter and fun. Or it can help to visualize times in life when you feel grounded and safe, such as getting a big hug from your very best friend or sinking into bed at night, for instance. When you calm your heart, you can recover your balance and reclaim your healthy joy.

In discovering the patterns in your second number, you probably recognized more than one way you experience them. Just gaining an awareness of these tendencies can empower you to respond differently. Before, you were likely to have been immediately lost in your feelings, and it could have taken quite some time to return to balance. But now you can be more conscious of when your emotional self starts to take over and respond in a new way.

Your emotional self shows up when you become upset or stressed. It's like the image you sometimes see in cartoons: a little person standing on your shoulder, whispering in your ear. That person will always be talking at you during these times, but now that you're aware of the themes in what they're saying, you're totally in charge of how seriously you listen. Instead of taking what they're whispering to heart and getting swept out into your emotional sea, you can respond with a calm attitude, almost like a parent saying, "There, there, honey, everything will be all right." As you practice that, you'll soon find that these feelings come up, are felt, and then move on while you're standing in balance, and all is well.

Let's move on to examine your third number for a full understanding of the invisible design of your personality and purpose in the world. Now that you know the patterns in your overall nature and your emotional self, you can look at your work in the world, including what lessons you came here to learn and your special calling in life.

CHAPTER 5

YOUR LIFE CHALLENGE AND YOUR TRUE CALLING

Now we arrive at your third number, which unveils more of your unique hidden nature and weaves into your other two numbers to create your symmetry, the beautiful design that is you!

Your third number shows how you come across when you first meet someone, and it also reveals how you do your work in the world—as well as how you do anything, really. We look at the third number to see what kinds of careers might be fulfilling in addition to those indicated by your first number, and to understand your approach to doing anything such as planning your weekend or tackling a project.

But there is an even more important pattern revealed by your third number, and it has two sides. On one side, it reveals your life challenge, that pattern of problems that you'll continually bump up against in big and little ways throughout your life. Until you learn its theme, you may not even be aware of how all these problems have the same underlying symmetry. But now you can start to connect the dots and see how this pattern keeps appearing, from small daily problems to major issues that repeat over the decades.

At the same time, when we look on the other side of this pattern, we discover what the Chinese call your destiny or what we might define as your *true calling*. It represents your greatest power, your ultimate strength, and it's what you're evolving toward. You see, your life challenge—the pattern in all these problems you encounter along the way—isn't bad. It's actually what provides you the stepping-stones that lead the way to your ultimate goal. It's only by working through this set of challenges that you can achieve your calling.

One of the reasons I have such respect for this system is that it's not a cookie-cutter approach. This is a sophisticated understanding of the human spirit that honors its unique complexity, and there's a glorious variety of ways it can be expressed. So in the following sections, I'm not going to wave a magic wand and proclaim, "X is your life challenge, and Y is your true calling!" Instead, I'll describe the essence of the pattern for each number, and it will be up to you to observe and recognize how it shows up in your life and to understand where it's leading you. You may immediately see a few ways it's been a part of your experience and where it's been leading you, but the more you ponder and observe over time, the more connections you'll see. What I find for most people is that once they learn to see the pattern, they discover it showing up on a daily basis, both as their challenge and their growth into their calling.

I want to remind you that we're only looking at your third number here; for instance, if your numbers are 7.2.1, you would read the section about One.

Third Number: One
Wisdom of the Ancestors

Because the One nature tends toward silence, it's likely that someone's first impression of you will be that you're rather quiet or self-contained. You may even come across as mysterious and intriguing, with a magnetic charm that invisibly draws people to you rather than your reaching out to grab their attention.

In terms of how you do things, your need for freedom and independence will take precedence here. You prefer to just wake

up on Saturday to see what you feel like doing that day, not to have it all planned out in advance. You don't like restrictions or to be tightly scheduled, and you'd love to have the power to do things differently every time, depending on your mood!

Life Challenge

This is the issue that's woven through your life, appearing repeatedly in both subtle and obvious ways. If One is your third number, fear can be a frequent pattern of experience. It may be that a major phobia interferes with your life, or that fear is the emotion that tends to block you time and time again. Some people who have this pattern even try to use fear to intimidate or bully others.

You may also be resisting your natural psychic ability. In our culture, intuition is considered weird and "woo-woo," and you might be afraid you'll be ostracized if you make it known, so you try to suppress it or keep it secret. It can also be scary to really open to the information that could be coming to you. You may worry that you're going to start seeing dead people (or more dead people than you already are!) or that you'll be hearing so many messages in your head that you won't be able to handle it.

If this feels true, your work is to find ways to embrace your intuitive nature because it's your power, not your problem. Don't wander through it alone. Get training, advice, and guidance so that you can develop your skills and own this part of yourself.

Qualities of secretiveness are associated with the energy of One, so you may tend to be a very private person in general or even carry a secret that you struggle with over decades in your life. This same pattern can support an attitude of suspicion or even paranoia; for instance, you may think that someone has underhanded motives whether or not they actually do.

It wouldn't be unusual for a part of your life challenge to center around issues of abandonment—a fear of people leaving you. Based on their actions, you may be quick to conclude that they have abandoned or ostracized you when in fact that might not be true. It could also be that you have repeated experiences of abandonment, and your work is to stay whole and healthy despite them.

The influence of your ancestors can be an issue for you; there may be some disharmony that you've inherited down through your family line that you're trying to heal without being aware that the problem didn't originate with you but possibly generations before. It can be a real eye-opener to explore this possibility, and many people find it's a huge relief to see how they may have been carrying family karma but judging it as their personal issue. Just that knowledge can be incredibly liberating and allow you to relate to your life experience in a new way. If this theme of inherited issues resonates for you, therapy, energy clearing, or a form of energy work called Family Constellations may be worth exploring.

Other ways the One nature may challenge you are through a struggle with your need for freedom and flow in how you live or dealing with the consequences of your choosing an unusual lifestyle. Because the energy of One has to do with deep emotions, you may need to learn to manage how you're swept away by your feelings or find ways to not lose your voice when you're upset.

Your Calling

Because the One influence makes you creative, your career may be in the arts, especially music or radio (because hearing is governed by the qualities of the One); or you might paint, write, or act. However, your innovative mind can also be brilliant in the fields of science, medicine, or finance. You might end up in an unusual career or do your work in unconventional ways or at odd hours, or your job may involve international travel.

You're intuitive and have a natural healing ability, so you could earn your living as an intuitive counselor or healer, holding a powerful space for clients to deal with their deepest and most intense feelings.

Ones are attracted to mystery, so you might have a career as a mystery writer, magician, or shamanistic healer. Along with this comes a special interest in death and dying, so work in end-of-life care and counseling—such as a funeral director or as a genealogist—are options as well.

There's an aspect of the One nature that has to do with risk and danger, such as jobs with FEMA, other work involved with helping after a disaster, or a career that involves danger and adventure. Finally, people with a One as their third number can find themselves in fields dealing in some way with water—for instance, being a plumber, sailor, spa owner, or swimming instructor.

What the Chinese call your destiny, we might understand as your true calling, the highest power you're evolving toward. When a One is in this position, it signifies that you were born with wisdom in your bones, and your greatest strength is all within. It's by developing your inner talents and abilities that you achieve your purpose, not by chasing new knowledge. Your job is to deepen and build on what you already have. That doesn't mean you shouldn't study and learn from others, but that you apply what you learn to strengthening the deep power within.

The journey here is about learning to trust the process. The more you think you have to make something happen or find the answer elsewhere, the farther you travel from your greatest source, which is that deep inner flow. You have the strength of all the ancestors behind you, supporting you, and all you have to do is allow that essence to give you power, courage, and wisdom.

Third Number: Two
Divine Feminine

On first impression, people will notice your kind, helpful nature, a sweet energy about you that lets them know you're on their side. It's likely that upon first meeting someone, you'll be

concerned with their comfort in some way, whether it's giving them the best seat or offering them a snack, or in a more subtle way, such as steering the conversation to be all about them.

In terms of how you do things, you're thoughtful and want to help. Unless your other numbers modify this one, you're not likely to be a risk taker, and you strive to complete whatever project you're working on because you'd hate to let someone down. You're the one others can rely on to stay with something till it's finished and to be sure everything's taken care of. You may not like to be rushed or pressured in your work, and you have the potential to get a bit too bogged down in all the details, so extra time lets you go at a slower pace that will allow this.

Life Challenge

This is the issue that's woven through your life, appearing repeatedly in both subtle and obvious ways. If Two is your third number, the theme of your challenge may center around taking care of other people. It may be that you're overly responsible and too other-directed, so you continually sacrifice your own needs to help everyone else or too often act as a rescuer. At the same time, it's possible that life arranges to put you in this position so that it's less of a conscious choice and more what you've been handed to deal with.

But either way, it's essential to work on your boundaries. It can help to visualize Mother here, which represents the Two nature. The stereotypical matriarch is always on call, tending to her family's needs and putting her own needs last. But if Mother works herself into the ground and doesn't take care of herself, then she's no good to anyone. She needs to learn to be able to set limits—to say no sometimes and not feel guilty about it. A healthy mom can delegate, ask for help, and accept it when it's given.

If Two is in this position for you, you may have a pattern of over-giving and/or under-receiving, and it will be your job to work on bringing that ratio into balance. Part of this involves watching

how often you fall off your own to-do list in favor of taking care of others, rather than exhibiting good self-care. It may be that you sacrifice your needs or feel so obligated when anyone asks you to do something that you accept the task even if you don't want to. You might feel guilty when you do something you enjoy, worried that you're being selfish. You could have the mind-set that you have to do the work all by yourself, and the thought of asking someone to pitch in doesn't even occur to you. Or like a resentful mother, you feel that even if someone does help out, you just end up having to do it over again because they didn't do it right, so you may as well take care of it yourself the first time!

So you'll also need to be mindful of just how receptive you're being. People may be trying to help, but you may not recognize their efforts because you're carrying expectations about what that assistance has to look like. Perhaps your disappointment that nobody ever steps up to lend a hand has given you such a negative attitude that no one wants to try anymore. Occasionally, someone with a Two in this position isn't aware of how much they've started to sound like a victim—nagging, complaining, or feeling sorry for themselves—and people begin to react unkindly or just tune them out.

Because the energy of Two also represents home and putting down roots, there could be a struggle with being able to feel a real sense of home for yourself, or you might not feel connected with a community of friends as much as you'd like to. Personally and professionally, you can be uncomfortable having to go it alone. If you run your own business, you'll long for someone to collaborate with. In your personal life, you may yearn for a partner you can come home to and share your day with. At the extreme, people with this quality even seem needy or selfish, or their partner complains that they demand support but don't offer the same in return.

You may also have had a difficult relationship with your own mother when you were growing up that still affects you today, even if your experience with her has improved. This pattern may also be expressed as challenges concerning being a parent yourself. For instance, one woman who never wanted to have children but got pregnant accidentally says that being a mother was profoundly transformational and made her everything she is today.

There can be issues with low self-confidence; while these feelings will always come up for you, you're completely in charge of how seriously you listen to them. It's really your conscientious nature showing, but too often you can let worry slow you down or keep you stuck.

Finally, do watch for tendencies to give away your power. This is a more extreme version of the pattern of over-giving, one in which you may disempower yourself to try to build up someone else, allow someone to dominate you, or loyally stay in an unhealthy relationship long past the time you should have left.

Your Calling

You may find that no matter what your job description is, people tend to come to you for support, and you're also likely to be the one always offering to help because it feels so natural to do so. Anything from administrative support all the way to upper-management positions is a good fit because you take such great care of everyone, and your compassionate approach makes people happy to work for you.

Other possible careers could be in real estate because one theme here has to do with home; another theme is food, so you might excel as a chef or nutritionist. You may even end up as a collector because this influence has to do with accumulating wonderful objects that bring you pleasure.

You can be an excellent teacher because you're so good at feeding information in the ways your students need to receive it. Since you're naturally devoted to helping others, careers in psychology, social work, nursing, or caregiving can also be fulfilling.

What the Chinese call your destiny, we might understand as your true calling, the ultimate power you're evolving toward.

When your third number is a Two, your purpose in life is to become what can be defined as the Divine Feminine, that strong compassionate presence that offers a safe and accepting embrace for anyone, no matter who they are. This energy has nothing to do with being masculine or feminine; instead, it has to do with the spirit of devotion.

In Chinese culture, this is the essence of Quan Yin, the Taoist goddess who's the embodiment of mercy, love, and compassion, yet is also a fearless protector. It's believed that her name originated from the Sanskrit word *Avalokitesvara,* which can be translated as "the One Who Hears the Cries of the World."

You're here to hold a powerful place for others, one that's soft and receptive but at the same time is also the strongest source of safety. You're able to allow the truth of someone's being and still stay grounded. Your journey in life is toward achieving this powerful way of service without ever becoming a servant.

Third Number: Three
Agent of Change

People will find you bright and enthusiastic on first meeting and may consider you quite outgoing, although that could change as they get to know you better, depending on what your other numbers add to the mix. You'll probably appear confident and ready to take action if needed, although some individuals can perceive you as too ready, even a bit pushy, depending on their own personalities.

In terms of how you do things, you like to stay organized. You'll be the one to have the weekend all planned out by Friday because it just makes sense that way. You'll value the logical approach to anything and appreciate structure in life, with to-do lists and a well-organized home and office.

Life Challenge

This is the issue that's woven through your life, appearing repeatedly in both subtle and obvious ways. The basic theme here has to do with a push upward, like plants sprouting through the ground in the spring. This energy is the drive to be alive, that sense of urgency of something wanting to be born.

This push is so strong in nature that a tiny green shoot can break through concrete. For people, it shows up as Warrior energy, ready to launch into action. Your first thought may be to do, to go for it, rather than sit and think or wait and see. That strong drive can be perceived by others as pushy or aggressive behavior, when to you, it's obvious that action is required, so let's get on with it! There can even be such a compelling urge to act that you disregard others' needs or do something impulsive that you later regret. You may at times blurt things out without thinking about others' feelings, be confrontational, or be too competitive and driven to win.

There is the potential for being judgmental here, leaping to conclusions about others without giving them a chance. Alternatively, you may feel so worried about the judgment of others that you keep your head down and hinder your own progress.

You'll probably react in frustration and anger too easily, or even struggle with depression. And unless your other numbers modify this, your impatient energy can incline you to be a bit twitchy, to only be able work on short-term projects, or even to struggle with attention disorders such as ADD/ADHD. This can also be experienced as compulsiveness—for example, workaholism or compulsive exercise—or a hyper-focus that means you can't stop playing computer games far into the night. It also creates the potential for addictive tendencies.

Another way Three energy can be understood is as the Elder. This is anyone who's in a superior position, such as an older family member, a boss, a teacher, or a mentor, and who has power over you in some way. When Three is your third number, it might signify that someone who falls into the category of Elder has abused that power over you. It may be that they tried to dominate you, shamed you, or in some way expressed their authority in an unkind way. This might be an experience with one person that affects you for the rest of your life or a series of incidents with different people over time, where you feel like someone tries to take away your power. An example of this is a father who wants to "make a man" out of his son and so is very hard on him to toughen him up. But this often manifests itself as abuse, plain and simple.

If this does happen, the result can be a person who has issues with authority and who goes around with a chip on their shoulder. It may mean that they try to dominate in their own relationships, or it can be that they carry a great fear of ever being shamed or blamed. This can even affect relationships in small ways, the most frequent one being that they may rarely be able to say, "I'm sorry," even if they were at fault; or they'll blame everyone else rather than own up to being responsible for a problem, which feels too much like admitting weakness.

If this is true for you, just being aware of the origin of this pattern can help ease it, but there's also a need for forgiveness. One starting point is to recognize that the unkind elder was emotionally damaged. No one who was healthy in their heart of hearts would have ever behaved that way. The process of allowing that truth can be the beginning of letting go of pain and anger, which will allow you to move forward in a whole new way. And of course the essential part of this process is being able to forgive yourself for any misguided thoughts that you were somehow responsible for or deserving of mistreatment.

Your Calling

In terms of career, you'll enjoy any work that lets you be physically active, such as athlete, personal trainer, or massage therapist. You like structure and authority, so you may be attracted to careers in law enforcement or the military. Politics could appeal because you're driven to effect change in the system.

You also love to be active mentally, so a career as an analyst, engineer, or inventor is an option; or you might be an attorney because you're so talented at logical argument and debate. People with a Three here are often found in the business world—especially as entrepreneurs, because of their bright ideas and competitive drive. Other careers that align well are architect, landscape designer, gardener, carpenter, or woodworker.

One special talent you have is getting people up off their rear ends, and combined with your ability to strategize, this means you can be a fantastic personal coach. You can help people create a vision for their future and a plan to get there, and then keep them moving forward toward their goals. You won't coddle them—in fact, you may push them a bit hard—but they'll thank you for it in the end!

What the Chinese call your destiny, we might understand as your true calling, the ultimate strength you're evolving toward. The powerful drive of your Warrior energy shows you the way to your purpose, which is to be a catalyst, an agent of change for the world. The true calling for the Three nature is to create positive change, to see what's wrong and fix it, and to break up the old ways of being to make way for the new.

In our culture, we usually think of anger as a bad emotion because we're surrounded by its negative and destructive expression. But when you look at the root cause of anger, in its heart, it's really just a desire to change something that's judged to be wrong. Healthy anger is the same inner force as your drive to grow and develop; it's actually your booster rocket to make you take action, to be a benevolent force in the world.

Third Number: Four
Gentle Influence

On first impression, you come across as easygoing and gracious, someone who makes space for others to be themselves. But people may also feel a bit unsure about where they stand with you. To them, you may seem evasive, as if you might change at any moment and the ground isn't even firm under their own feet when they're with you.

In terms of how you do things, your Four nature is flexible. While you'll always have a plan, you'll also want a plan B, so you're able to adapt to changing circumstances. There may be a pattern of wavering or uncertainty overall, which can lead to procrastination, changing your mind, or overconcern with timing.

Your Challenge

This is the issue that's woven through your life, appearing repeatedly in both subtle and obvious ways. One image for the Four nature is bamboo. The bamboo bends with the wind; it's very flexible and adaptable to changing conditions, which is a great benefit. But that can mean you struggle to choose just one direction and stay with it, feeling indecisive, hesitating, or getting distracted in ways that don't serve you well.

This can also be seen in the tendency to overthink everything. It's hard to act on a decision because as soon as you've decided, you start to doubt that choice and may back off, thinking of new things to consider. You can get so wound up in your head that you feel flustered and unable to trust your decisions, or you could be too easily influenced by the opinions of those around you.

You can be too hard on yourself, beating yourself up for every little mistake, or for not being able to move forward as easily as everyone else seems to. You carry a natural drive, an inner tension that if not released through action can cause frustration and even anger. Over time, this can be internalized to eventually transform into depression, which is anger turned inward.

To counteract this tendency, get out of your head by staying active physically—go for a hike, play sports, do anything to release that inner tension. The joking advice, "Don't believe everything you think!" definitely applies here.

Because your bamboo nature bends to all of your thoughts and to others', too, there's also the risk of gullibility—too easily believing what someone tells you. In my experience, however, this soon flips to the opposite attitude, which is skepticism. You might feel suspicious of someone's motives and be too quick to assume that they have an agenda or are trying to trick or cheat you. To you, it may just seem as though you're being realistic, but you can lose opportunities when you're too doubting. Adding to this problem is a tendency to be judgmental or to jump to conclusions before giving others a chance. Tapping into your common sense will help, as will bouncing your thoughts off grounded friends.

The influence of Four can make you think the grass is greener somewhere else, so you can move, choose new jobs or relationships, or just change your mind too often. But life will also naturally bring you changes in career and lifestyle, and you may have to come to terms with that—it might help to work on releasing the belief that you should stick with one job and collect the gold watch 50 years later, for instance.

Your issues around timing can create trouble with procrastination or too great a concern about doing things at exactly the right time. You might get started but then keep changing things or even drop a project because you're feeling uncertain about the outcome.

Your Calling

To you, it's essential to keep growing throughout life, to continue to learn and improve yourself; therefore, you'll be a lifelong student. One of the most valuable things you can do is find mentors —people who are farther down the path than you are—to guide you, teach you the ropes, and possibly open some doors for you.

The theme of changeability is a major influence on your career, and you may have many different jobs or work in various places over the years. Because of your inherently flexible and gracious nature, you would be an excellent manager of a staff of any size. Your talent for guidance means that you could find success

as a coach or consultant. You never push; instead, you're a gentle hand on someone's back, just aiming them in the direction they need to go but always able to correct the course, depending on how things unfold.

You can do well in fields that have a bureaucratic structure, such as government or corporate work, because you're adaptable enough to fit in but not feel trapped; you appreciate and can work with the system. And your idealism can translate into work in philanthropy or with organizations that are fighting to make the world a better place.

Other careers might be in the art world due to your creative talents; out in nature, such as gardener, landscape architect, or ecologist; or working with wood, such as carpenter. And because one theme of the Four nature is wind, you might find happiness as a pilot or flight attendant.

What the Chinese call your destiny, we might understand as your true calling, the ultimate purpose you're evolving toward. Your power is like that of a gentle breeze, influencing but never forcing, to help others achieve the perfect balance of adaptability with forward movement so they can soar and glide through life.

The patterns in Four energy are associated with how plants grow. Most people think plants just shoot up and up and up in a vertical line, but time-lapse photography reveals that they bend and wobble in that upward movement, adjusting to changing circumstances and unfolding their inner plan in more of a spiral. This is your truth: to be a benevolent influence for growth and change, using your skills for gentle yet never-ending movement to guide us all in the direction we need to go.

Third Number: Five
Centering Force

Here's an interesting thing about Five: If your third number is Five, the other two numbers in your sequence are identical. If you look at the chart at the end of Chapter 2, you'll notice that whenever the third number is a Five, the first two numbers are the same. Take a look—you'll see: 1.1.5, 2.2.5, 3.3.5, 4.4.5, and so on.

For the most part, the influence of the Five here is like tofu, soaking up all the other flavors in a dish. When a Five is your third number, therefore, it takes on the characteristics of the other two numbers. This is much like when Five is the second number, where it transforms almost completely into the other numbers.

But here, when it's the third number, there can still be a minor influence from the Five nature, usually appearing as involvement in helping others or ending up at the center of things personally and professionally. It will make you a more powerful force in whatever you do, and people can perceive you as strong but demanding.

Overall, when your third number is Five, we'd put more weight on the meaning of the other two numbers because the Five does take on their essence. So if your numbers are 1.1.5, your third number actually is considered to be more like a One, as if you're a 1.1.1, and in order to learn what your challenge and calling are, you'll read the section about Ones earlier in the chapter. If you're a 2.2.5, that Five becomes more like a Two, as if you're a 2.2.2, and you'll read the section about Twos; and so forth.

There's one exception: If you're a 5.5.5, brace yourself! You've taken that "force of nature" energy of the Five and tripled it. When it comes to first impressions, what someone initially perceives about you is also who you are overall: an incredibly kind, generous person who's intent on helping, but who also demands people's attention.

In terms of how you do things, you'll tend to want to be in charge, because it's been your experience that you're just better at figuring things out than most of the population is. Yet do be aware that others can perceive this behavior as controlling or demanding.

If you're a 5.5.5, your life challenge might come from an extreme childhood that requires you to do a lot of personal healing work over the years. It can also center around the frustration of not having enough people in your life who really "get" you and with whom you can have the kind of solid relationships you so yearn for. And you may find that time and time again, you show up to provide powerful help but get relatively little recognition or appreciation in return.

A life lesson can, in fact, revolve around healthy boundaries. You may do too much for others and feel guilty whenever you take time for yourself. But this challenge can also show up for some Fives as their invading others' boundaries by being demanding, sticking their noses in other people's business, or trying to "help" by taking charge when it's not appropriate.

Such strong Five energy can also give you extreme emotions, which you may have to learn how to manage, although some Fives are in such fear of their power that they stay emotionally shut down as a result.

When you're a triple Five, there will usually be drama from family and/or friends to contend with, and you'll probably be the one required to step up to help. You tend to be the center of gravity for everyone in your life, so this shouldn't be a surprise! You may often feel as if people don't really see how much you did for them, though, and you should take care to not get stuck in disappointment or resentment.

As for your calling, you're so adept and resourceful that you're capable of doing anything you want. You'll be intensely drawn to helping others no matter what career you land in, and anyone who has a triple Five in their life has a powerfully nurturing supporter.

Third Number: Six
Sacred Connection

The first impression you make will be as someone with excellent manners, but because the Six carries a sense of power and authority, people may also get a feeling that you're a bit aloof or even arrogant, and you may need to compensate for that by being extra warm and approachable.

In terms of how you do things, you like to feel in control. It's best for you to know what to anticipate in any situation, and the earlier you get the details, the more comfortable you'll be. Some people with this number here may drive others crazy with discussions like whether the dinner reservations should be at 6:30 or 6:45 for your first night at the hotel . . . on a trip that's six months down the road.

Your Challenge

This is the issue that's woven through your life, appearing repeatedly in both subtle and obvious ways. If Six is your third number, it could revolve around issues of perfectionism and self-worth. One way to understand it is as having "enough" issues: You have a concern about being good enough and doing things well enough, which can create a constant undercurrent of anxiety. You may procrastinate because you're so afraid you won't do it right; or you may be highly self-critical, cringing at every perceived mistake no matter how inconsequential. God forbid anyone offers you constructive criticism.

For some, the anxiety about "enough" can extend beyond issues of self-worth to a worry about money, and as a result they pinch every penny no matter how full their bank account may be. Alternatively, some put a high value on affluence and impressing people, even if the show they put on isn't one they can really afford. This challenge around "enough" can also be expressed in relationships. For example, perhaps they grew up without receiving enough affection and so don't know how to give it; their partner may complain that they're not affectionate or don't understand the importance of gifts.

A Six in this position creates a high level of sensitivity to subtle energy, which can make you physically uncomfortable in large crowds or noisy environments, or you may need to have things just so—to control them in an attempt to manage the overwhelm

that can occur for someone with such a sensitive side. This can create difficulty in relationships, with your partner saying that you're nitpicking or trying to boss them around. It helps to be aware of how others might experience your behavior in ways you didn't intend.

Another reason you may insist on things being done your way is the influence of the essence of the Six, which is the energy of Father. He holds the power in the family and is to be obeyed! You may carry a natural air of authority and an expectation that what you say goes, and that can rub some people the wrong way. It can also incline you to be inflexible at times, unwilling or unable to see others' viewpoints or consider their needs.

At the same time, your challenge may be about being able to stand in your power. There's often a longing to feel worthy of respect, yet often any praise you receive bounces off while criticism soaks in deeply. This may have roots far back to a difficult relationship with your father in childhood, when you felt as though you weren't good enough for him. As an adult, it can cause you to seek approval from powerful people.

The essence of the Six energy is that of heaven or the Divine, a sense of the sacred. You'll feel drawn to do work that feels sacred to you, that is meaningful and will make a difference in the world. You may disdain material wealth or even feel disgust for people who lead shallow, superficial lives. To you, authenticity is of utmost importance, and it's key to have relationships where you can be your true self.

You could have a pattern of holding on to grief, of not being able to let go and move on after a loss. Instead, you might keep looking back at what you've lost and so relive the pain over and over, reluctant to turn forward for fear that there will be nothing there. It may be difficult to believe the reality that out of your losses there can come a new resolve and that you can face the future not diminished but empowered.

Your Calling

In your career, you may end up in a position of power, such as CEO, politician, or some other type of leader. But no matter what you do, when you show up to work, you take charge. You're a natural visionary, able to see the kind of life we could all achieve if we weren't so caught up in all our little dramas. Your idealism directs you into work that feels sacred, so you might have a career as a clergy member or spiritual teacher, able to inspire people to connect with their divine nature.

But along with seeing the big picture, you're exquisitely aware of the tiny details, so careers that require precision are also good, such as surgeon, acupuncturist, accountant, or engineer. The Six sensitivity can direct you toward work that requires an awareness of subtleties, from energy work to interior, graphic, or fashion design.

What the Chinese call your destiny, we might understand as your true calling, the ultimate power you're evolving toward. Your true purpose is simple: to live a sacred life. Your calling is to bring an elevating energy to the world, inspiring us all to a higher awareness and our best lives.

Honor your need for authenticity and meaning in your career, relationships, and lifestyle. Work on establishing healthy energetic boundaries so you're not buffeted or knocked off balance by the invisible currents swirling around you. If you can do this, you'll move to a place where you can hold great power within your own life and for others.

With the breath in and the breath out, you always come back to this moment of perfection, where you can let go of grief and find the treasure—which is how deeply you've been enriched by all your experiences, each moving you more fully into the sacred.

Third Number: Seven
Creation of Beauty

You're an absolute charmer on first meeting, gracious, witty, and able to make anyone feel welcome. People may get the impression that you're affluent whether or not you actually are, and you may be surprised that they behave a little deferentially at first.

In terms of how you do things, you'll be concerned with others' needs in any situation and very willing to alter your plans so that everyone can be happy. True to your perfectionist nature, you'll focus on getting all the details right and worry that what you do won't be good enough.

Your Challenge

This is the issue that's woven through your life, appearing repeatedly in both subtle and obvious ways. With a Seven here, there's always a self-critical streak that can make you feel uncertain about the rightness of your choices and cause struggles with issues of self-worth.

Highly aware and self-conscious, you can sense what's going on with the people around you, and you often feel too responsible for their experience. At times you may even tell little white lies, saying what you think the other person wants to hear even if it's not true. You do it to try to be nice, but if they later find out that it wasn't true, they can misunderstand and think you were insincere —or worse, that you were lying to them. You'd never view it that way. You were just trying to make them happy, and the truth may have been too uncomfortable a conversation for you to have.

It can help to understand this behavior by visualizing the image for the Seven: the glassy surface of a lake, which is perfect and without a ripple. The Seven influence here makes you continually work to have things as perfect and beautiful as possible. This also means being uncomfortable with conflict or confrontation and always trying to put a good face on things. If a problem continues unresolved, the Seven may avoid directly addressing it and instead fall into passive-aggressive behavior, or denial, hoping that if we all just pretend things are pretty, they really will be.

The energy of a Seven in this position inclines you to take your responsibilities too seriously, to let them weigh too heavily on your shoulders; and there's the chance that you'll deprive yourself of your own needs in the process. You can be overly conscientious or perfectionistic or too much of a good soldier, toughing out difficult times rather than asking for help.

Some people with a Seven as their third number live too minimally because of concern about money or alternatively become hoarders, accumulating piles of things just in case, unable to throw something out because they might need it. But there can also be too much attention on appearances, being status conscious or worrying about what people will think of them. Even if they're hoarders, it's likely that no one would ever know. From the outside, the house looks perfect.

One image for the Seven is the Princess. When it's in this third position, the image can be expressed as a longing to live the good life, to be taken care of and not have to work so hard. You may dream of your ideal days in a big, beautiful home, with few responsibilities and a charmed life. There's also the possibility that you actually do end up living a life of affluence and prestige, but it challenges you in some way. It's fascinating that Seven is the third number for both Diana Spencer and Sarah Ferguson, two women who greatly struggled with being princesses.

Your Calling

You excel in any field that requires attention to detail and awareness of how to make things beautiful. Work as a fine artist, jewelry maker, fashion designer, interior designer, florist, or graphic designer is all well suited to anyone who has a Seven in this position.

You could find success in the hospitality industry as a cruise director, concierge, maître d', or wedding or party planner. But this same quality can also be used in communications, writing, public speaking, research, languages, media, or the entertainment industry.

You work with precision and can deal especially well with money, so a job in the financial world can be a good fit. However, this same quality will incline you to be highly sensitive, and it can be a bit overwhelming to work in large institutions or surrounded by a lot of people. Add the Seven's "free spirit" influence here, and you may prefer to freelance no matter what career you choose, rather than being locked into one job or stuck in a busy office all day.

What the Chinese call your destiny, we might understand as your true calling, the ultimate power you're evolving toward. When your third number is Seven, your true purpose in life is to create beauty. At its heart, what this really signifies is your ability to appreciate the preciousness of every moment, the incredible beauty in every subtle detail of life around you.

You remind us to live with grace. You reflect what's pure and true and real inside us and help us remember what we value. Your calling is to bring a refined and gentle presence to the world, inspiring us all to become present, drawing our attention to this moment right now, and allowing us to feel how perfect and holy and beautiful it is . . . and we are.

Third Number: Eight
Deep Transformation

On first impression, you have a quiet warmth and a solid presence, and people will get an immediate feeling that they can rely on you. You may come across as overly serious; at the same time, others may sense that you don't feel entirely sure of yourself. But you'll also be the first one to volunteer to help in any situation.

In terms of how you do things, your attention is directed toward the needs of others. This doesn't mean you're a social butterfly—it's just the opposite, because you like your alone time. But a lot of your life will naturally revolve around your commitments or helping people in some way.

Unless the influence of your other two numbers modifies this Eight, you're not usually comfortable with being spontaneous; instead, you like to take your time to think things through. You feel it's silly to proceed with anything without a good plan in place, and you can sometimes be slow with that process.

Your Challenge

This is the issue that's woven through your life, appearing repeatedly in both subtle and obvious ways. If Eight is your third number, this can involve your natural generosity and drive to take care of others. You may take on too much responsibility, or life may just arrange to give it to you. Either way, you can work too hard, too long, or too seriously and may lose all sense of yourself in the service.

You feel drawn to supporting others. It might be that as a child, you were more the parent for your own mother; or that you take care of her or even both parents as they age, or even other family members on and off throughout your life. But if this isn't part of your experience, others (both friends and family) will still naturally choose you to ask for help, and there can be no end to your work. While you sincerely do want to show up for people, you also have a strong personal need for your own space. Remember, Eight is associated with the image of the cave inside the mountain, and you'll need to balance helping your tribe with time when you retreat to pay attention to your own self-care.

It can be hard to say no when you need to and not feel selfish about time for yourself. If the balance of giving and receiving falls too far out of whack, you can begin to feel resentful and eventually angry. That mountain can turn into a volcano, blasting the people in your life with your upset at being used, taken for granted, or unsupported. It's really a lifelong process, this work to develop healthy boundaries and not feel so responsible for everyone's welfare. You'll always feel pulled to be the one to step up, but you're not at the mercy of this impulse. You can learn to manage the feeling and recognize the yin and yang of it—when it's okay to give and when it's time to stop and ask someone else to pitch in.

The issue isn't just about attending to whether you over-give, but about how receptive you are as well. These are two halves of the same cycle, and you tend to be brilliant at being the giver but not so great at opening your arms to receive. You'll have to work on allowing others to lend a hand and even (gasp!) asking for help so that the people you've given so much to know how to return the favor.

You can respond with enormous anger to issues of unfairness and can be single-minded in your determination to get justice for yourself or for others. It's possible to get stuck and just keep digging yourself deeper into the problem rather than finding a way to resolve it and move on.

The qualities of Eight are hard work, reliability, and diligence; and you may repeatedly choose situations that require all those characteristics and then some. You can wonder why you always seem to end up doing things the hard way or why life can't be as easy for you as it is for some. But what this is really about is the essence of the Eight, which is transformation. You choose experiences that create struggle because it's only through hard work that true inner change can be achieved. You aren't here to coast; you came to gain deep knowledge and achieve powerful inner growth.

Your Calling

As a for career, the Eight influence makes you take your work very seriously, and you can succeed at whatever you put your mind to through pure diligence and determination. Someone with an Eight in this position often does very well as an entrepreneur because of this. There's also a theme of accumulation here, which can mean accumulating wealth (often through deliberate effort, not overnight success) or working with finances, such as in the banking industry or estate planning.

Because of your drive to help others, other jobs that would be a natural fit include social worker, nurse, business manager, or caregiver of any sort. With that pillar-of-strength mountain characteristic, you give powerful help, often for large groups rather than just one person at a time. If you own a business, you'll treat all of your employees like family and go out of your way to make sure that everyone is well taken care of.

In the mountain, there is a cave; and the cave is where the knowledge is, so you might be a teacher or consultant. But the cave is also where transformation happens, so work as a member of the clergy or psychologist can be fulfilling as well.

Since a hot button for you concerns issues of unfairness, other careers are mediator, attorney, union organizer, or community activist, working to ensure that everyone's rights are protected.

The themes of home and the land apply here, so jobs such as real estate agent or appraiser, property developer, or property manager can be good. Many people with an Eight as their third number dream of establishing a retreat center where groups of people can go to focus on spiritual growth. There's also a pattern centering around food, so a career as a nutritionist, chef, or restaurateur is a possibility.

What the Chinese call your destiny, we might understand as your true calling, the ultimate power you're evolving toward. When your third number is Eight, your purpose in life is to be that mountain of strength and knowledge, offering your deep understanding of how harmonious the world can be if only we can each stand in our truth.

You help call us home to our deep desire for our tribe, our loving community of family and friends that gives us a safe place to land. But most of all, you offer yourself as a wise and nurturing support, taking our hands, guiding us deep within, and helping us through a powerful alchemical process to discover our own buried treasure.

Third Number: Nine
Fearless Heart

The first impression you make is as a warm, friendly, and outgoing person. There will be a sparkle about you, and others will assume that you're an extrovert, but they may be totally wrong. People with a Nine in this position will shoot their energy out to someone on first meeting, but their true nature may actually be shy and introverted, depending on what their other two numbers are.

In terms of how you do things, you like freedom and spontaneity instead of being locked into some rigid schedule. You'll make any project fun and always bring a lighthearted attitude to whatever you do. It can feel too heavy to be around people who don't respond when you crack a joke or try to make things fun.

Your Challenge

This is the issue that's woven through your life, appearing repeatedly in both subtle and obvious ways. Nine is about the heart, which you will definitely wear on your sleeve. Rejection can be an issue for you—whether it's the hurt you feel if someone doesn't return your affection or because you're so frightened of rejection, you hold yourself back and miss opportunities. You may have lessons around understanding that it's not possible to be special to everyone and to not take it personally if someone doesn't respond in the way you'd hoped.

Others may judge you as being flamboyant or wanting attention because you're so expressive. This is a misperception, but it can cause problems in relationships. You may not realize you're putting some people off when you're merely being your lit-up self!

You think fast and learn quickly. In fact, depending on the influence of your other numbers, you may do everything fast, with words tumbling out of your mouth more rapidly than people can follow. But along with this comes a tendency to speed overall, and that can mean you have trouble completing projects. You'll get excited about something and you'll stick with it while it's still fun; as soon something else grabs your attention, though, you may drop the old project for the new one.

The influence of the Nine can also mean that your heart is so open that you can be overly trusting of others in general or that you can let someone get too close too soon and end up getting hurt. There may even be a pattern of experience that's usually recognized as betrayal. Sometimes this can be in romance with an unfaithful lover; but it can also show up in other ways, such as with a business partner or family member. You may not have specifically defined it as a betrayal at the time, but looking back, you can see that's really what it was. One woman's husband failed to file their tax returns for ten years and lied to her about it, for example. It was a huge shock when she discovered warning letters from the IRS hidden in the bottom of his desk drawer.

In Chinese medicine, your consciousness is believed not to reside in your brain, but in your heart. If you have a Nine here, this means that you have an open consciousness as well as an open heart, and you're affected by what others are thinking and feeling. You may know who's calling when the phone rings, but what also happens below your awareness throughout the day is that the thoughts and feelings of other people affect your own. This tendency to be a "psychic sponge" can cause you to develop a constant background anxiety, as little energetic messages float in from the person working on the other side of the partition in the office or sitting next to you on the plane and blend with your own thoughts and emotions. I always recommend training in intuition and energy work so that you can begin to develop better psychic boundaries and transform this empathic ability from a challenge to a strength.

Your Calling

As for a career, it's possible that you'll end up in the spot-light, your work involving being seen in some way. Especially since you're creative and a natural performer, you could be happy as an actor, singer, artist, or public speaker. But you also have a talent for getting people inspired and excited, so other careers could include sales, marketing, public relations, or communications. Since you have a special talent for making people laugh, your work will be done with humor—you could even become a comedian.

You'll do best in a career where you interact with others rather than work in isolation; it's also essential that your job be fun because the moment you're bored, you'll want to move on. The travel industry is an option because it gives you the opportunity to see new places and meet new people, your favorite things.

What the Chinese call your destiny, we might understand as your true calling, the ultimate power you're evolving toward. We might simply say that you're here to develop a fearlessly open heart. Maybe it's easiest for me to explain by sharing my own story, since my third number is Nine. Decades ago, when I first began to work with feng shui, I started to notice that at the end of every consultation, my clients were making the same comment. I remember the day it dawned on me what this meant.

I was feng shui-ing the home of a woman who shared her story with great embarrassment, hardly looking me in the eyes, as if she were ashamed of what she was saying. She described how she'd conquered alcoholism through sheer force of will and then had struggled with and overcome a serious eating disorder. At this point, she was unemployed and depressed; on top of that, her husband had come to her and said that he'd always felt like a woman trapped in a man's body, so he'd decided to have sex-reassignment surgery but hoped she'd stand by him. She sat there with her eyes downcast and quietly said that she'd given it a lot of thought and had realized that since she truly loved her husband, it shouldn't matter whether he was a man or a woman, so she'd decided to stay in the marriage.

I sat across from this woman, breathless, in total awe of her heroic journey. She'd fought so hard to heal herself, and despite her current emotional downturn, she was able to stay in her heart and continue to love her husband. After I was finally able to speak, I quietly reflected back to her the genuine strength, beauty, and courage that I saw in front of me. She was finally able to hold my gaze, and I hoped she really was hearing my words.

We went on to feng shui the house. When we were saying good-bye at the end, she said to me the one sentence I'd kept hearing from person after person in my feng shui work: "I feel like you came to my house and fell in love with me."

Wow, did my heart sing, and with a flash, I realized that was my true calling in life! This is really what my work has always been about—with feng shui, face reading, Nine Star Ki, and energy clearing—I'm in the business of falling in love.

If this is your number, too, your work is to develop your own fearless heart, to hold a place of pure love in the world. It doesn't mean that you stay wide open emotionally and let yourself get hurt, but instead that your heart has such healthy boundaries that it can genuinely dance with the energy of anyone you encounter and still be safe. It's easy to say but not so easy to do, and the real work is always to open your heart to yourself.

Recognizing how your third number is expressed in your own life can help you move beyond your old limitations to embrace what you used to perceive as problems. Now you can understand them as lessons that are leading you further toward your greatest purpose. You may have discovered how yearnings you've felt throughout your life for a certain kind of work, lifestyle, or relationship have a powerful meaning within the context of your third number. With this knowledge, you may find ways to more easily reach your heart's desire!

As you've seen, this seemingly simple set of three numbers reveals an intricate world of meaning. The very best way to integrate what you're learning is to not only practice applying it to yourself, but also to use it in your experiences with others in real-life situations. The three numbers interact and influence each other in a unique and harmonious symmetry, just like all things in nature. The more you work with this system, the more you'll see how it gives you a deep and thorough understanding of anyone's true spirit.

However, you don't always have to analyze at length in order to discern important information about someone. You can learn to get a glimpse of anyone's patterns from their particular three-number design. In the next chapter, I'll give you some examples to demonstrate.

CHAPTER 6

81 Combinations

In order to understand someone, you need to consider all aspects of their personal hidden symmetry—all three of their numbers and how they dance together. The effects of some qualities can be modified by the influence of others, so it's important to remember that the numbers all interact. For instance, if someone is a 6.2.9, their Nine can make them reach out to someone in their desire for a heart-to-heart connection. But as soon as they've made an intimate contact, their Two's lack of confidence and their Six's sensitivity to that person's energy can kick in and make them pull back. This can be a bewildering experience for the other person . . . unless they've read this book!

What follows are brief descriptions of each of the 81 different Nine Star Ki combinations to help you start to see ways the qualities can interact. When someone is in balance, they'll live the healthy version of their numbers; if they are out of balance, however, the expression becomes unhealthy. Each section gives you brief snapshots of both so that you can learn to identify where someone is in their personal evolution. I've also included some examples of noteworthy people with those numbers. You'll most likely recognize them as famous names from the world of self-empowerment; along with celebrities in entertainment, sports, or politics.

Of course, these are very abbreviated readings and show only a sampling of the ways these influences can weave together. To really understand someone, read the descriptions for each of their numbers in the previous chapters and then observe how these characteristics play out in your experience of them.

A note about twins: Because twins share the same birth date, they have the same Nine Star Ki numbers, but of course they have different personalities, so you might wonder how this system could have meaning here. Yet what you'll find is that while they'll both carry the essence and influence of their numbers, one twin will be the yang version of these qualities and the other will be the yin expression. In other words, the yang twin will be the more active and outgoing version of their numbers, more externally expressive; and the other will show the more introverted and quiet side of the same characteristics, more focused on their inner world. Every parent of twins whom I've worked with has immediately been able to identify which one is the yang twin and which is the yin.

Interestingly, I've worked with three sets of triplets over the years, and in every case, they recognized one sibling as the yang version, one as the yin, and for the third they all agreed it was as if that one had been dropped in from outer space—totally different in personality from the other two!

1.1.5

Healthy expression: You're born with natural intuition, deep willpower, and a strong need for freedom and independence. Highly creative, you'll probably live an unusual life. You have a magnetic personality and can develop your inner strength to help others do the same.

Unhealthy expression: You have the potential for arrogance, secretiveness, or suspicion.

Famous examples: Jennifer Hudson, Serena Williams, the Reverend Al Sharpton

1.2.4

Healthy expression: You have an adaptable and caring nature, and people find you easygoing and very likable. You may be artistic, yet cautious in life overall; even after you choose a direction, your life path just naturally involves lots of change.

Unhealthy expression: You can let fear and self-doubt block your progress.

Famous examples: Whitney Houston, Beyoncé Knowles, John McCain

1.3.3

Healthy expression: You have a creative nature and an idealistic desire to change the world, and people may be surprised by your incredible drive and determination. If you can tap into your strong inner discipline, you can achieve all your goals.

Unhealthy expression: You can be too direct and disregard others' feelings.

Famous examples: Nelson Mandela, Jack Kornfield, Pema Chödrön

1.4.2

Healthy expression: Your gentle way of being belies your deep inner strength. You always want to help others and are willing to patiently set your own needs aside to do so. With your creative nature, you're sure to find ways to express your artistic side.

Unhealthy expression: You may struggle with self-doubt or give away your power to others.

Famous examples: Johnny Depp, Natalie Portman, Kris Kristofferson

1.5.1

Healthy expression: You have a deep emotional nature and incredible willpower. Your need for freedom and independence will factor into every decision you make. Highly creative and intuitive, you might live the life of an artist or healer.

Unhealthy expression: You may be overly ambitious or secretive and ruled by fear.

Famous examples: Priscilla Presley, Mike Myers, Wayne Brady

1.6.9

Healthy expression: You're a creative free spirit, independent and adventurous. Warm and gracious with others, you can put anyone at ease. But you're not always extroverted—you also benefit from regular times of solitude.

Unhealthy expression: You can feel overwhelmed and anxious, especially if life goes too fast.

Famous examples: Michelle Obama, Jackie Chan, Jet Li

1.7.8

Healthy expression: Thanks to your imaginative nature, you may end up working in the arts. You love private time because that's when your creative juices flow. There's a lot you may not say in order to spare others' feelings or because you don't believe they'd understand.

Unhealthy expression: You can be insecure, secretive, or stubborn.

Famous examples: Brad Pitt, Quentin Tarantino, Mary Tyler Moore

1.8.7

Healthy expression: You need your space in life, and regular solitude is like vitamins for you. You can power through difficult times with your deep inner strength. You have a natural charm with people because you're so good at reading them.

Unhealthy expression: You may have secrets or just say whatever you think people want to hear.

Famous examples: John Travolta, Ron Howard, Bette Midler

1.9.6

Healthy expression: You're intuitive and sensitive, with insights other people lack, and because of this you can be a very inspiring influence. You'll have a strong vision of what to do in any situation and care about doing things right.

Unhealthy expression: You can be obstinate or try to manipulate people.

Famous examples: Jenny McCarthy, John Lithgow, Henry Winkler

2.1.6

Healthy expression: Kind and caring, you highly value family and all your relationships. You'll be able to take charge when necessary and do whatever needs to be done. You have an emotional depth others may not recognize.

Unhealthy expression: You may act like a victim or hold on to hurt feelings far too long.

Famous examples: Ewan McGregor, Rosie O'Donnell, Diana Ross

2.2.5

Healthy expression: You feel compelled to help others and may end up at the center of a movement or organization, even as you struggle with self-confidence. You want deep and long-lasting friendships and will invest time and energy in all your relationships.

Unhealthy expression: You can be critical or controlling or feel sorry for yourself.

Famous examples: Chelsea Clinton, Woody Allen, Martha Beck

2.3.4

Healthy expression: You want to make the world a better place and will do best working within an organization to gently change the system from the inside rather than being a rebellious activist. People respond to your kind, gentle nature.

Unhealthy expression: You can get lost in self-doubt, overthink things, or struggle with depression.

Famous examples: Thich Nhat Hanh, Tony Shalhoub, Winona Ryder

2.4.3

Healthy expression: You have an enormous drive to be of service, and you can be a real force for change in the world. You can help motivate people to create a new vision for moving forward in life and keep them headed in the right direction.

Unhealthy expression: You may struggle with frustration, anger, or depression.

Famous examples: Louise Hay, Amma ("the Hugging Saint"), Lance Armstrong

2.5.2

Healthy expression: You're kind and generous, with a sincere desire to do good work. It will be important to you to establish a good home and have lifelong friends. Your attention will always go toward the needs of others, and you enjoy being a source of support for those you care about.

Unhealthy expression: You can criticize and complain or act like a victim.

Famous examples: Lyndon Baines Johnson, Alfred Hitchcock, Steve Carell

2.6.1

Healthy expression: You work hard on any project because you care so much and want to get it right. You need freedom and flow in life, yet you honor your responsibilities and devote time and energy to authentic connections with friends and family.

Unhealthy expression: You may expect others to take care of you without doing much in return.

Famous examples: Elisabeth Kübler-Ross, Kristi Yamaguchi, Wesley Snipes

2.7.9

Healthy expression: You're warm, affectionate, and attuned to communicating in ways people can understand. Your strong sense of devotion can move you toward careers involving helping others, especially ones that center around teaching. Your life may revolve around your work.

Unhealthy expression: You're hypersensitive and may sacrifice yourself for others to the extreme.

Famous examples: the Dalai Lama, Benazir Bhutto, Tom Cruise

2.8.8

Healthy expression: Incredibly loyal and caring, you have a quiet depth of strength and provide a sense of safety and stability for the people in your life. You can work long and hard and will always be the one to help the underdog.

Unhealthy expression: You can be judgmental and resistant to change.

Famous examples: John F. Kennedy, Marilyn Monroe, George Lucas

2.9.7

Healthy expression: You have a sincere desire to help others and make them happy, and you're far more sensitive to people's energy than they may realize. Charming and gracious, you can excel at inspiring people to live better lives.

Unhealthy expression: Your responsibilities may feel too heavy, and you struggle with perfectionism and a sensitivity to energy.

Famous examples: Oprah Winfrey, Howard Stern, Justin Timberlake

3.1.7

Healthy expression: You're energetic and enthusiastic and can easily charm people to your benefit. You're more sensitive and emotional than others recognize. Highly creative, you'll want to use your ideas to make the world a better place.

Unhealthy expression: You overreact to criticism and may be driven by the desire for status.

Famous examples: Princess Diana, Liam Neeson, Ricky Gervais

3.2.6

Healthy expression: You're driven to prove yourself and want to feel proud of your achievements. When you get down to work, you manage any self-doubt and then really take charge and attend to all the details so that things are done and done well.

Unhealthy expression: You can be competitive, judgmental, or critical.

Famous examples: Tina Fey, George Clooney, Katharine Hepburn

3.3.5

Healthy expression: You have a powerful vitality that draws other people's attention. You're very goal oriented, and it's important to you to stay active. You'll always feel driven to learn, grow, and achieve and may help others do the same.

Unhealthy expression: You may struggle with anger, depression, or addiction.

Famous examples: Elvis Presley, Jim Carrey, Kate Hudson

3.4.4

Healthy expression: Your gentle, adaptable nature helps you work well with people; and you may assist others in improving their lives. Your active mind can think of more than one solution to any problem. If plan A doesn't work, you have B and C ready to go.

Unhealthy expression: You can be skeptical, judgmental, or challenged by depression.

Famous examples: Gloria Steinem, Queen Latifah, Mariah Carey

3.5.3

Healthy expression: You may be a catalyst for others; you don't coddle people but get them moving again toward positive growth. Your logical mind can see what's wrong in the world, and you'll feel a strong drive to change things for the better.

Unhealthy expression: You can struggle with anger, depression, or addiction.

Famous examples: George Harrison, Caroline Myss, Meg Ryan

3.6.2

Healthy expression: You're driven and dedicated, with firm ideas of what you want from life. You have the energy to achieve your goals and the patience to finish what you start. Relationships will give you important lessons.

Unhealthy expression: You can be selfish or demanding and sensitive to criticism.

Famous examples: k. d. lang, Margaret Thatcher, Jeff Goldblum

3.7.1

Healthy expression: Highly creative, you're ambitious and driven, yet you always honor your need for freedom. Your vitality and determination can take you far—and as you trust your intuition, life can carry you to interesting places.

Unhealthy expression: You may be stubborn, pushy, or ruled by fear.

Famous examples: Pink, Julio Iglesias, Chevy Chase

3.8.9

Healthy expression: With your strong personality and powerful energy, you're able to inspire and motivate others. You combine a logical approach with warmth and enthusiasm, and your focused drive helps you achieve your goals.

Unhealthy expression: You can be judgmental, pushy, or impulsive.

Famous examples: Robert De Niro, Jay Mohr, Roger Waters

3.9.8

Healthy expression: You're a hard worker, and your focus may be on helping others or making the world a better place. If you combine your logical mind and intuitive insight with your single-minded determination, you can accomplish great things.

Unhealthy expression: You can be a workaholic or struggle with anger.

Famous examples: Barack Obama, Mick Jagger, Marianne Williamson

4.1.8

Healthy expression: You have an adaptable nature and an emotional depth others might not recognize. You're a hard worker with high moral principles, and you'll be a lifelong student, always looking for ways to develop yourself.

Unhealthy expression: You can be skeptical, judgmental, or lack self-confidence.

Famous examples: Jimmy Carter, Sting, Zach Galifianakis

4.2.7

Healthy expression: An excellent communicator, you're witty and charming with other people, able to make everyone feel welcome. As you learn to manage your perfectionism, you empower yourself to create a beautiful life and feel proud of your accomplishments.

Unhealthy expression: You can overanalyze, procrastinate, or be too self-critical.

Famous examples: Sean Penn, Antonio Banderas, Jack Black

4.3.6

Healthy expression: It's important to you to feel proud of your achievements, and you may rise to the top within a structured system. You'll always be focused on getting work done and learning new things, and you don't like to waste time or effort.

Unhealthy expression: You can be cynical or easily frustrated with others.

Famous examples: Harrison Ford, Amelia Earhart, Jennifer Lopez

4.4.5

Healthy expression: You have an easygoing, diplomatic nature, and you may be influential in your career. An excellent thinker and an idealist, you can use your analytical ability to help others. Life will be full of change and growth.

Unhealthy expression: You can be indecisive or suffer from anger or depression.

Famous examples: George H. W. Bush, Paul McCartney, Rupert Sheldrake

4.5.4

Healthy expression: You idealistically work to make the world a better place, and you can easily deal with a variety of personalities. Life will take you in many different directions, and you're adaptable enough to deal with all the changes.

Unhealthy expression: You can be moody, overthink everything, or deal with depression.

Famous examples: Bono, Anne Heche, Kristin Scott Thomas

4.6.3

Healthy expression: You're focused and goal oriented; with your logical mind, you really can get things done. You work hard to do things right, and you can adjust your plans to suit changing circumstances, always looking to the future.

Unhealthy expression: You're too hard on yourself and can be challenged by fear of others' judgment.

Famous examples: Carol Burnett, Janis Joplin, Barbra Streisand

4.7.2

Healthy expression: You're kind and sensitive and adapt easily to others' needs, always aware of what they're feeling. Naturally artistic, you have good common sense as well; you'll feel drawn to helping others no matter what job you do.

Unhealthy expression: You tend to overthink everything and doubt yourself and others.

Famous examples: Albert Einstein, Michael Eisner, Katie Holmes

4.8.1

Healthy expression: You combine a powerful mind with a creative and intuitive nature, and you'll always need freedom in how and when you do your work. You'll experience change throughout life, but can stay centered through all that movement.

Unhealthy expression: You can struggle with self-doubt, anger, or depression.

Famous examples: Byron Katie, Jennifer Aniston, Javier Bardem

4.9.9

Healthy expression: With your bright spirit and great sense of humor, everyone likes you on first sight, and you can make people feel uplifted and inspired. If you focus consistently to complete projects, you could make real progress.

Unhealthy expression: You can deal with depression or anxiety, or repeatedly put everything into a project only to have it all fall apart.

Famous examples: Jean-Claude Van Damme, Kathy Griffin, Sanjay Gupta (neurosurgeon)

5.1.9

Healthy expression: You're a people magnet with a big personality, and your emotions are even more powerful than others realize. You're driven to get to the top in your career and may end up in the spotlight.

Unhealthy expression: You can be controlling or have an insatiable need to be the center of attention.

Famous examples: Lady Gaga, Howard Hughes, Celine Dion

5.2.8

Healthy expression: You're a powerful force in the world, always drawn to helping others, and you have a strong need for connection and community. Incredibly generous with your time and energy, you'll always work hard at whatever you do.

Unhealthy expression: You can constantly create drama or be extremely demanding.

Famous examples: Elizabeth Taylor, Daniel Craig, Margaret Cho

5.3.7

Healthy expression: An excellent communicator, you're very charming—if you wanted to, you could wrap anyone around your little finger. Family and relationships are very important to you, and you need to create a beautiful home to enjoy them in.

Unhealthy expression: You may manipulate or use people to get what you want.

Famous examples: Hugh Jackman, Marie Osmond, Sarah Ferguson

5.4.6

Healthy expression: You're driven to achieve big things and can hold a powerful place in the world. It will be important to you to earn the genuine respect and recognition of others, and you'll work hard to feel that you've reached a certain level of success.

Unhealthy expression: You may be controlling and demanding in your desire for power.

Famous examples: Mohandas Gandhi, Will Smith, Jesse Jackson

5.5.5

Healthy expression: You are a force of nature, resourceful and resilient and with a powerful need for authentic relationships. As you learn to accept your power, you can do great work, which for you will always center around helping others.

Unhealthy expression: You may feel vastly unappreciated, and your anger can be epic.

Famous examples: Magic Johnson, Shaun White, Rachael Ray

5.6.4

Healthy expression: It will be key for you to do something important in the world, especially to right wrongs or improve others' lives. Life may take you in different directions, but in the midst of change, you'll always want a sense of rootedness.

Unhealthy expression: You can be demanding and controlling or act without integrity.

Famous examples: Arianna Huffington, Richard Branson, Martha Stewart

5.7.3

Healthy expression: You have a powerful personality, with a strong drive and enthusiasm for living life to the fullest. You need to stay active, and it's good to always be thinking of what's next. Lifelong friendships are essential for you to feel fulfilled.

Unhealthy expression: You can try to dominate others or push too hard for what you want.

Famous examples: Lindsay Lohan, Kanye West, Hugh Laurie

5.8.2

Healthy expression: You're a generous friend, and it's important to you to stay connected to a community of people who you feel really know and appreciate you. You love to help others and are especially thrilled when they act on your advice.

Unhealthy expression: You can be a know-it-all or needy and selfish.

Famous examples: Stevie Wonder, Robert Pattinson, Nora Ephron

5.9.1

Healthy expression: You're creative and strong willed and need to express your talents in order to feel fulfilled. You want freedom in how you live your life, but at the same time will always need a sense of stability.

Unhealthy expression: You can be demanding and may behave without integrity.

Famous examples: Muhammad Ali, Ashley Judd, Jay Leno

6.1.1

Healthy expression: You're intuitive and creative, and you'll want to do things your way—not only because you care so much about the quality of your work, but because you're so independent. You can develop into quite a visionary in your field.

Unhealthy expression: You're insecure, fearful, and can have secret agendas.

Famous examples: Prince, Nicole Kidman, Meryl Streep

6.2.9

Healthy expression: You have the potential to become an authority with your work, and it will be important to you to achieve a certain level of power and recognition. Life will offer you key lessons about managing your sensitivity in order to reach your goals.

Unhealthy expression: You can be narcissistic, arrogant, and dismissive.

Famous examples: Wayne Dyer, Colin Farrell, Drew Carey

6.3.8

Healthy expression: You have high principles and work hard to achieve your goals. With your idealistic nature, you place a lot of value on doing the right thing. It can be frustrating to work with people who are less aware than you are.

Unhealthy expression: You can be arrogant, controlling, or disdainful.

Famous examples: Ram Dass, Michelle Pfeiffer, Dick Cheney

6.4.7

Healthy expression: You're charming and sensitive to others and put a lot of care into everything you do. You may go back and forth on decisions before you settle on a direction, but then you can be sure it's the right one.

Unhealthy expression: You can be critical, controlling, or status-driven.

Famous examples: Rupert Murdoch, Edgar Cayce, Alec Baldwin

6.5.6

Healthy expression: Highly aware, you're sensitive to the subtleties and nuances in any situation and care about each little detail of a project. As you learn to manage your sensitivity, you can achieve your goals and even hold a place of authority and power.

Unhealthy expression: You may be overly sensitive, controlling, or critical.

Famous examples: Bonnie Raitt, Kurt Cobain, Jeff Bridges

6.6.5

Healthy expression: You're a leader, not a follower, and carry a natural sense of authority. It will be important to you to feel you've earned the respect of others and that you've done quality work. You have the potential to be a visionary in your field.

Unhealthy expression: You can be demanding, controlling, or hypersensitive.

Famous examples: John Lennon, Anna Wintour, Julia Roberts

6.7.4

Healthy expression: Your idealistic and perfectionistic nature makes you care very much about doing things right. You have a gentle charm with other people and will always strive for meaning and authenticity in relationships and your life in general.

Unhealthy expression: You can overanalyze, and be both critical and self-critical.

Famous examples: Desmond Tutu, Sigourney Weaver, Bruce Springsteen

6.8.3

Healthy expression: Your focused drive can land you in a position of power, and it's important to you to do something special with your life. With your high principles, you don't want to waste your time on small talk or superficialities.

Unhealthy expression: You can be judgmental, arrogant, or disdainful.

Famous examples: Madonna, Michael Jackson, Richard Gere

6.9.2

Healthy expression: Your kindness and warmth makes it easy for people to immediately like you. You have a strong sense of obligation; it's important to you to do a good job. Relationships will teach you important lessons.

Unhealthy expression: You can lack energetic boundaries or be controlling.

Famous examples: Martin Sheen, James Brolin, Philip Seymour Hoffman

7.1.2

Healthy expression: You're attuned to the energy around you and can make anyone feel welcomed and appreciated. Extremely sensitive, you'll notice subtle things about people, and you're naturally drawn to helping others with what you observe.

Unhealthy expression: You can be hypersensitive and too cautious, or lack confidence.

Famous examples: Kate Winslet, Avril Lavigne, Fran Drescher

7.2.1

Healthy expression: Your quiet charm and sincere desire to make things better for people serve you well personally and professionally. You're intuitive, creative, and highly aware; and it's best to have freedom in how you do your work.

Unhealthy expression: You can be insecure, fearful, and challenged by indecisiveness.

Famous examples: Julia Child, Lily Tomlin, Sean Connery

7.3.9

Healthy expression: Creative and expressive, you're an excellent communicator with a good sense of humor and natural warmth. While you shouldn't choose a career that keeps you isolated, you also need regular solitude and lots of freedom in your work.

Unhealthy expression: You can be emotionally reactive or manipulative.

Famous examples: Charlize Theron, Garry Trudeau, Cat Stevens

7.4.8

Healthy expression: You have high standards and work very hard to achieve the results you want. Extremely aware, you're a kind, caring friend. Your career may involve helping others, although you'll always need to do your work your way.

Unhealthy expression: You can lack confidence or get blocked by insecurity.

Famous examples: Frank Lloyd Wright, John Cusack, Julianna Margulies

7.5.7

Healthy expression: You're articulate and charming and can read other people well, which makes you an excellent communicator. You have a natural sense of style; and as you learn to manage your sensitivity, you'll enjoy creating a beautiful life.

Unhealthy expression: You can be critical, controlling, or highly anxious.

Famous examples: Angelina Jolie, Russell Brand, Janet Jackson

7.6.6

Healthy expression: Your quiet reserve may belie your high level of awareness. You have a lovely way with people, and your work is always beautifully done. As you learn to manage your perfectionism, you no longer hide your light under a bushel.

Unhealthy expression: Your perfectionism and hypersensitivity can keep your life too limited.

Famous examples: Richard Nixon, David Beckham, Ellen DeGeneres

7.7.5

Healthy expression: You're extremely charming and adept at creating wonderful experiences for people, no matter what your career. With your high level of sensitivity, you pay great attention to details and focus on making everything as perfect as possible.

Unhealthy expression: You can be controlling and anxious or present a false front.

Famous examples: J. Edgar Hoover, Tiger Woods, Steven Tyler

7.8.4

Healthy expression: You have a sincere charm and people naturally feel comfortable with you. You want to make a real difference in the world; with your high standards, you can achieve powerful results with your work.

Unhealthy expression: You can be judgmental and easily frustrated.

Famous examples: Drew Barrymore, Gordon Ramsay, Scarlett Johansson

7.9.3

Healthy expression: You're creative, expressive, and witty, and this can take you far. It will be important to you to feel you've achieved something meaningful and important—and as you learn to manage any anxiety, there's no stopping you.

Unhealthy expression: You can be highly anxious or manipulative.

Famous examples: John Cleese, Katy Perry, Ralph Lauren

8.1.3

Healthy expression: You're ambitious, hardworking, and a very loyal friend. Driven and devoted to doing good in the world, you can use your determination and strong will to accomplish powerful results that can potentially help large groups of people.

Unhealthy expression: You can be easily frustrated or act childishly.

Famous examples: Elton John, Glenn Close, Ryan Seacrest

8.2.2

Healthy expression: With your generous nature, you care very much about everyone being treated fairly, and work hard to support the people in your life. You like to put down roots and need a community of like-minded friends.

Unhealthy expression: You can be judgmental and take things too seriously.

Famous examples: Ronald Reagan, Leonardo DiCaprio, Ben Stiller

8.3.1

Healthy expression: You have the wisdom and willpower to push through difficult circumstances and do powerful work in the world. You'll always need solid relationships and a sense of home, but you also require plenty of alone time on a regular basis.

Unhealthy expression: You can be antisocial or struggle with anger and obstinacy.

Famous examples: Hillary Clinton, Eleanor Roosevelt, Carrie Fisher

8.4.9

Healthy expression: You're warm and caring; while you take your work seriously, it will also be important to you to have time for fun. You may achieve some level of fame, but you'll still need regular private time.

Unhealthy expression: You can be insecure and too much of a pleaser.

Famous examples: Amy Winehouse, David Copperfield, Jimmy Fallon

8.5.8

Healthy expression: You're incredibly kind and generous to family and friends, and all your relationships are important to you. You learn from your mistakes in life—they only deepen your growing wisdom—and you're driven to share what you've learned with others.

Unhealthy expression: You can be judgmental, angry, or reclusive.

Famous examples: Charlie Sheen, Kenny Rogers, Kim Cattrall

8.6.7

Healthy expression: Your kind sincerity combines with a deep sensitivity to give you a lovely presence with people. Strong willed and dedicated, you'll work hard to help others. You find that life becomes easier as you learn to manage your boundaries.

Unhealthy expression: You can be anxious, perfectionistic, and controlling.

Famous examples: Jacqueline Kennedy Onassis, Tom Hanks, Arnold Schwarzenegger

8.7.6

Healthy expression: You'll want to live a meaningful life and make the world a better place. It will be important to you to always have a sense of the sacred, and you have the ability to inspire others to live their best lives as well.

Unhealthy expression: You can be arrogant, critical, and demanding.

Famous examples: Anne Frank, Randy Jackson, Salman Rushdie

8.8.5

Healthy expression: You have enormous inner strength and are a nurturing presence for everyone in your life. You'll always look for opportunities to help make things better for others, and you have the patience to set your own needs aside to do so.

Unhealthy expression: You can be too driven, stubborn, and judgmental.

Famous examples: Brooke Shields, Alanis Morissette, La Toya Jackson

8.9.4

Healthy expression: You come across as quite easygoing and charming, and you have a generous spirit and caring heart. You will be a lifelong student and will want to share what you learn to make the world a better place.

Unhealthy expression: Your strong emotions can cause impulsiveness or poor choices.

Famous examples: Audrey Hepburn, Katie Couric, Penélope Cruz

9.1.4

Healthy expression: You're personable and fun loving and naturally attract attention, yet you feel things more deeply than others may know. Life will bring lots of change, but you'd be bored if it were any other way.

Unhealthy expression: Lust for fame can negatively affect your judgment.

Famous examples: George W. Bush, Donald Trump, Sandra Bernhard

9.2.3

Healthy expression: It's important to you to live your passion, although you may not stick with things long-term because you seek change and new challenges. It's better not to work in isolation because you need more stimulation than most people do.

Unhealthy expression: You can be overly emotional or aggressive.

Famous examples: Chow Yun-Fat, Wynonna Judd, Heidi Klum

9.3.2

Healthy expression: You're naturally warm and affectionate and have a passion for life. With your inherent ability to inspire people, you have the potential to teach them the important lessons you learn about compassion and acceptance.

Unhealthy expression: You may have trouble letting go of a relationship, or the other person could refuse to leave—to the point of stalking.

Famous examples: Martin Luther King, Jr.; Russell Crowe; Paula Deen

9.4.1

Healthy expression: You have a warm and easygoing presence, yet a delicate emotional nature. You'll always need change and variety, to experience new things in life, and to express your creativity.

Unhealthy expression: You can be insecure or overly sensitive to rejection.

Famous examples: Maya Angelou, Steven Spielberg, Jane Fonda

9.5.9

Healthy expression: Creative and expressive, you're driven to live your passion and spread love; if you can stay focused, you have the potential for great success. To you, nothing is worth doing unless it lights you up.

Unhealthy expression: You can be vain and manipulative.

Famous examples: Steve Jobs, Walt Disney, Marisa Tomei

9.6.8

Healthy expression: You want to achieve a level of power in life; because you're so motivated, you may well rise to the top. You're hardworking and dedicated, and people may be surprised by how seriously you take your work.

Unhealthy expression: You can be controlling or critical.

Famous examples: Bill Gates, Deepak Chopra, Maria Shriver

9.7.7

Healthy expression: Warm and gracious, you're very attuned to the energy of other people and sincere in your desire to make them happy. Everything you create will be beautiful, including the experiences you give to others.

Unhealthy expression: You can be anxious and need constant attention.

Famous examples: Yo-Yo Ma, Susan Sarandon, Tommy Lee Jones

9.8.6

Healthy expression: You're charismatic and driven to do something meaningful with your life, and you'll be single-minded in your desire to reach your goals. At the same time, you're a natural at inspiring others to do their best.

Unhealthy expression: You can be ambitious or unsympathetic to others.

Famous examples: Mother Teresa, Bill Clinton, Dustin Hoffman

9.9.5

Healthy expression: Extremely creative and passionate and with a love of stimulation, you may end up as the center of attention wherever you go. You're emotionally open, and this makes you a great friend to everyone.

Unhealthy expression: You may manipulate people or be a show-off.

Famous examples: Sandra Bullock, Courtney Love, Jimmy Smits

The descriptions in this chapter are only meant as brief examples, of course. There are many diverse and fascinating ways that you can express your unique nature. The more you can recognize your inner design, the more easily you'll be able to express it in healthy ways, and genuinely love and accept yourself. In the next chapter, we'll explore this even more deeply.

CHAPTER 7

YOUR ELEMENTAL NATURE

If you've read either of my books on Chinese face reading (*The Wisdom of Your Face* and *The Wisdom of Your Child's Face*), you know that all my work is based on the ancient principles of Chinese medicine, the foundation of which are the Five Elements, a system that evolved from further study of the harmonious movements in the circle of yin and yang. The Elements describe qualities of energy that represent how life works, the intricate patterns in nature. They're expressed as the terms *Water, Wood, Fire, Earth,* and *Metal,* and each of these is also descriptive of a certain personality type. In fact, if you've read my other books, most likely as you've been reading this one, you've been thinking, *That sounds a lot like a Water personality. This one sounds like a Wood person,* and so on. If you did, you were absolutely right!

Here are the basic qualities of the Elements:

— **Water:** This is the energy of winter, when it seems like nothing is alive on the surface, but in fact the seeds are germinating underground, unseen. It also holds the quality of nighttime, when you're floating in dream consciousness rather than dealing with the realities of life. And it's the mysterious land of both the time before birth and the afterlife, a dark and powerful place of creation and destruction.

— **Wood:** Here we find the energy of spring, an active time when the plants burst through the ground with a tremendous drive to be alive. It's also associated with morning, when we're feeling charged up and optimistic about the day. This is early childhood, that enthusiastic "go-go-go" energy of the little child running and shouting.

— **Fire:** Now comes summer, when flowers are in full bloom and the long days are full of sunshine and opportunities for fun. It also relates to high noon, the height of the day when the sun is at its brightest. This is the prime of life, that stage when you are at your physical peak and can't wait to get out there and look for love.

— **Earth:** This is early fall, harvest time, when the food is abundant and we can all rest easy. It's early afternoon, when you're back from lunch and just want to sit and not work so hard. And it represents middle age, when you begin to slow down and want to enjoy home and family more.

— **Metal:** Here is the last stage of the cycle, late fall, when the trees lose their leaves and it looks like all of nature is at the end of its life. It's like late afternoon, when you clear your desk to get ready to go home and rest. This is old age, when you appreciate the preciousness of each moment of the remaining time you have.

All of nature is made up of the Five Elements, even people. Each of the Elements has distinct qualities that reveal themselves in our personalities as patterns of tendencies to think, feel, and behave in certain ways; and with inherent values, beliefs, and reactions to the world around us.

Nine Star Ki is also based on the Five Elements, but was further refined and developed to show nine different personality types instead of the basic five. Like Chinese medicine, it's based on the *I Ching* or *Book of Changes*, which is one of the most ancient books in the world, said to be at least 3,000 years old. Although more commonly thought of in the West as a book used for divination, it actually offers a profound understanding of how life works, using eight patterns called *trigrams,* circling around a center axis. This is why there are nine numbers, one for each of the eight trigrams and the ninth for the center space.

Here, two things happen with the Five Elements: The names of the elements are expressed as numbers instead of words, and some of the elements are split into yin or yang versions.

The qualities of yin and yang are sometimes described as being feminine and masculine energy, but as you read in Chapter 1, there are many ways to understand their characteristics. And with people's personalities, these concepts have nothing to do with being like a woman or a man. To describe them very simply, a yang personality is one that's expressed outward or more actively, while a yin personality holds their energy inward or expresses it more tentatively.

Here is how the personality types are expressed in Nine Star Ki:

- **Number One** is the equivalent of a Water Element influence—creative, intuitive, deeply emotional, and with a lot going on under the surface.

- **Number Two** has what's referred to as a Yin Earth character. This is the pure Mother personality, whose life is all about nurturing others but who may give too much.

- **Number Three** is called Yang Wood, represented by the Warrior—enthusiastic, driven, and loving to be active mentally and physically.

- **Number Four** is Yin Wood, someone who carries a gentler version of the Warrior nature. You may have noticed some similarities between Three and Four in the descriptions earlier in this book, and that's because they're both Wood types.

- **Number Five** is also an Earth quality, similar to a Two but more powerful and grounded. You may have seen some parallels between Twos and Fives as you read, and this is why. Five is neither yin nor yang, but is considered to be the center that all the others revolve around.

- **Number Six** is Yang Metal, expressed as the powerful Father personality who's highly sensitive and aware because he's in charge of the family and needs to be sure all details are well taken care of.

- **Number Seven** is Yin Metal, also highly sensitive but much more attuned to adjusting to others' energy. Sixes and Sevens have a lot in common because they're both Metal; but as you've read, they have significant differences as well.

- **Number Eight** is Yang Earth, the third version of the Mother personality. This one is the mountain, the strong mother who's able to support a huge family; while the classic Two Earth has a softer, more receptive energy. The Five Earth, while still a giver, is more demanding of others' attention.

- **Number Nine** has the equivalent of the Fire influence—warm, expressive, and affectionate, yet overly affected by other people's feelings.

Even though your hidden design is made up of three numbers and not all nine, this doesn't mean that anything is missing. There's a perfect symmetry to how the qualities of your numbers weave together to produce your unique nature. We don't wonder why cats don't have wings or flowers don't grow fur! There's an intentional design to each creature in the world—reasons why they were formed the way they were—that allows them to function as planned and to live and learn what they're meant to in their time. You're a part of that same system. Your form has a coherence and meaning that's a perfect fit for who you came here to be.

Yin-Yang Relationships Among the Numbers

The yin numbers are Two, Four, and Seven; and the yang numbers are Three, Six, and Eight. One and Nine aren't split up into yin and yang versions; and as stated previously, Five is neither yin nor yang—it holds the center.

Having yin or yang numbers doesn't make you feminine or masculine; however, they do color your energy, affecting how you express yourself and how you come across to others. In our culture at this time, it can in fact be less comfortable for a man to have yin numbers or a woman to have yang numbers because they have qualities that our society defines as belonging to the opposite gender.

For example, if a man's first number is Two, he may sometimes feel as if somehow he's not manly enough, because the energy of Two is very yin, soft, and nurturing. A man who's a Two is completely masculine, of course, but is usually not dominating or over-competitive. Instead, he focuses on the harmony of the group, which is a wonderful quality in a man! In addition, if he's in a relationship with a woman who's a Six, for instance, he may feel controlled or even emasculated by her and blame her without recognizing the energetic dynamics of their partnership. The man is actually the yin Mother (Two) of the relationship while the woman is the yang Father (Six), the one in charge.

If a woman is a Three (Yang Wood), she'll be active, bright, and enthusiastic; but both men and women may judge her as a bit pushy or even aggressive. The energy of a Three is very direct and focused on action, certainly not the stereotypically sweet, shy girly girl; but this doesn't mean she's not feminine! However, she may sometimes feel bewildered by negative reactions from others when she's just being herself.

It can be such a relief to discover the influence of a yin or yang number on your personality and how others perceive you. It's not about trying to change who you are, but understanding why you're having this experience with people. Often just the awareness takes all the tension out and eliminates any chance of your blaming yourself for being who you are.

Differences within the same Element can even be challenging. For example, William was a Two married to Joan, a Five. Both numbers are Mother Earth personalities but with different flavors. Twos are the most receptive and even submissive of all the numbers, while Fives are quite powerful, even controlling and demanding.

William's perception was that Joan was always ordering him around, while Joan felt like she was a better problem solver than he and was just trying to help. Actually, both were true—she was only telling him what to do because she was more confident about being able to figure things out and wanted to support him. But Joan also exceeded boundaries at times and didn't let her husband do things his way. As a Two, William also lacked confidence, so her taking charge pushed all his buttons of self-judgment about that aspect of his personality.

The couple was invited to a dinner party, and Joan brought a homemade pie as a gift. The hosts had already prepared a dessert, but after dinner they graciously brought out both sweets for people to choose from. The host was at the head of the table, trying to dish up the pie but having a bit of trouble, when Joan leapt to her feet and took the knife from his hand, saying, "Oh, let me help you!" At that point, William turned bright red and shouted, "*Will* you let him do it?!"

The other guests had merely seen someone trying to help. Yet in William's mind, he was watching Joan control and emasculate another man, just as he felt she did to him, and he was horribly embarrassed.

Discovering how the influence of your birth date affects your relationship can be incredibly liberating and can help prevent misunderstandings or heal past ones to ensure smoother sailing going forward.

The various characteristics interact in many ways, of course—more than just yin and yang reacting to each other. A Three will want to leap into action, while a Six will want to triple-check first

to make sure every detail is right. A Two will place more value on personal connections, while a One will prefer to rely on their own inner resources. The key is to deepen your understanding of each of the numbers so that you can recognize and respect where someone's feelings and behaviors are coming from. In the next chapter, we'll explore just how important that is.

CHAPTER 8

FEELING SEEN

When Lisa met with me for a reading, I could tell she had a certain outcome in mind: She was determined to get permission to divorce her husband. It turns out that she'd been married for 25 years and had been miserable for most of them. She said it was obvious they were such different people in every way that they never should have gotten married, and there was no hope that they could continue to live in the same house together. They fought bitterly each day, and she knew that only by escaping this terrible union could she find happiness.

Of course, I could never tell Lisa whether or not to stay in her marriage. All I could do is share with her what I was seeing about her inner nature and that of her husband, and hopefully give her insights that would allow her to make the best decision for herself.

As I looked at the Nine Star Ki chart, my eyebrows went up—my client and her husband had the exact same numbers! She sat there expectantly, waiting for me to confirm their deep differences, but instead what I relayed to her was how alike they were.

When two people have the same numbers, they usually either get along like gangbusters or push each other's buttons. In romance, it often starts out seeming as though you've found your soul mate. But over time, this can transform into an experience where that person reflects back to you all the unloved parts of yourself, so they trigger you—and, of course, you trigger them, too.

As I did the reading, we explored how Lisa was expressing her inner design and how her husband's perceptions, feelings, and behavior were actually a version of the very same thing.

We talked about how the reactions between them had accumulated layer by layer over the years to bring them to this point. It didn't mean Lisa shouldn't get a divorce, but these new insights had taken away the story she'd been using to justify her desire to leave. However, even though we were able to come up with some options, I could tell that she continued to feel shocked by this turn of events since she'd arrived intent on an entirely different answer.

The next morning, Lisa called me, saying that she just had to share something with me. She said, "I left your hotel last night, got into my car, and sat there and sobbed for half an hour. I couldn't believe what you'd told me. I couldn't accept that my husband was anything like me at all. I felt totally hopeless.

"It was late, so I finally had to just go home. My husband had already gone to sleep, and I crawled into bed and lay there beside him, staring at the ceiling, feeling utter despair. As I lay there in the dark, listening to him breathe, it suddenly dawned on me— we *are* the same. He and I are the same. We want the same things; we see the world in the same way. His fears are my fears, and he craves love the same way I do. It was like my mind opened up and light streamed in. All the ways I'd been judging him were just a mirror of the things I hated about myself. All the things I blamed him for, I was doing the same as well. And in that moment, I knew that I had to heal this relationship. If I left now, I'd be in pain the rest of my life."

Lisa stayed in her marriage for five more years, devoted to learning to love herself *and* her husband. They finally parted, but they did so with respect and kindness, and she went on to live a joyful life, rather than spending years trying to recover and probably re-creating the same experience all over again with someone else.

Several years later, I heard from Lisa. She said she wanted me to know that she remembered the reading she'd had with me as the first time in her life that she felt truly recognized and accepted. She believed that experience was what made her able to go on to do the same for her husband as well.

I sometimes recall Lisa when I do a reading for someone, because there's often a moment at the end of our time together when the woman or man I've been working with gets up to leave, but then stops, looks at me with their face glowing, and says, "This is the first time in my life I've felt truly seen."

That's when I feel a rush of honor. I'm so grateful to have been able to give them that gift. Even though we probably talked about some tough stuff, even though I'm certain to have reflected to them how they've been getting in their own way, they didn't feel judged but recognized. Seen.

When I was writing *The Wisdom of Your Child's Face,* I did a lot of research on the latest findings in Western theories of child development. One of the most compelling studies I discovered was about how you can actually predict a child's future success based on one particular aspect of their parents' behavior toward them. It's not what you'd think—it doesn't depend on how often parents praise their child or how many times they say, "I love you."

In fact, the single most important predictor of a child's happiness and success is how much they feel *recognized* by their parents. If they feel their parents understand and acknowledge who they are, they have a genuine sense of acceptance, love, and connection. They feel free to be themselves for the rest of their lives.

Yet I don't think this ends in childhood. I think we all yearn to feel truly seen by the people in our lives, and it's even more important to be able to see ourselves with love and acceptance as well. This work gives us that gift. Knowing that there's a hidden symmetry to your personality allows you to step out of all the old limiting ways you've been viewing yourself and reclaim your true spirit. Just like everything else in nature, there's an inherent grace, rhythm, and purpose to you and to your life that's beautiful and right. And in the next chapter, Louise Hay gives you affirmations to help you embrace your true nature and live with joy.

CHAPTER 9

LOUISE HAY'S AFFIRMATIONS FOR YOUR TRUE NATURE

As you recall, the ancient principles in this book are the result of research over thousands of years that developed a sophisticated map of how all of life works, and that can be applied to any system to see if it's complete and true. In the Introduction, I described my amazed discovery that these principles completely validate Louise Hay's work with affirmations. If you lay the map of the Five Elements and Nine Star Ki over the structure of her work, each affirmation is a perfect fit for one of the nine numbers.

So Louise's information can be powerful here in supporting you as you move fully into the most joyful expression of your true spirit. The affirmations that follow were designed by Louise to help you remember who you really are and step into the beauty of your true nature.

Find the list of affirmations that matches your first number and choose one, two, or three of the phrases listed to work with each day. Select the ones that grab your attention or appeal to you the most, but also feel free to change it up and use other affirmations in that category, depending on what you sense you need at that time.

You don't have to only work with the affirmations that match your first number. You can use the affirmations for any of your three numbers in different ways. For example, if you're a 9.1.4, definitely use the affirmations for Nine—but if you're stressed or upset, you might also want to use the ones listed for the One nature, since that's who you become during those times. And when it comes to your career or the challenges you recognize as belonging to your third number, then turn to the affirmations listed for Four.

One

I trust the mysterious and unseen process of life. I know that I am safe and will be all right.

I have the inner reserves to overcome any problem.

I allow my deepest emotions, as they help me deal with all of the experiences I have during the day.

I become more proficient every day in every way. There are no limits to my abilities.

Today I just show up and flow through the day.

I have unlimited energy, and I use it well.

I am discovering new wisdom within myself.

I have the strength to remain calm in the face of change.

Opportunities are everywhere. I have unlimited choices.

I am in touch with my inner guides, who help me at every turn.

Life always reveals what I need to know, exactly when I need to know it.

I meditate each day. Going within helps alleviate tension and stress and allows me to hear what the Universe wants me to know.

What a great adventure my life is!

I have faith in the perfect unfolding of my life, and I can easily adapt to its ebb and flow.

Instead of isolating myself, whenever I need help, I ask. I accept assistance from my many seen and unseen friends.

Life is bringing me everything I need and more. My circumstances improve every day.

I welcome change; I do not fear it. I am always safe.

I easily handle any experience or situation that is put in my path.

I have the reserves to overcome any problem.

I trust the process of life.

Two

I attract loving, supportive people into my life.

My needs are always fulfilled.

I enjoy receiving help.

I love to help and feel satisfied by a job well done.

I take great pleasure in all the wonderful things in my home.

I am a grown-up, able to take care of every challenge that arises.

Life is very simple. What I give out, I get back.

I am open and receptive to all of the wonderful things in life!

I am comfortable enough to ask for what I want in positive ways.

I give myself permission to be a friend to others and a friend
to myself.

Everyone in my family is divinely protected at all times.

I am worthy of a healthy, intimate relationship with a
like-minded person.

I find relaxation and enjoyment in the simplest things in life.

I nourish myself by saying no when I mean no, and yes when
I mean yes. I know what I need.

I am patient, tolerant, and diplomatic. My words and actions
are kind.

I bless everyone in my life.

I am far more than other people's opinions. My opinion of
myself is the only one that counts.

I joyfully help wherever I can. Whatever I give out comes back
to me multiplied.

I give up the victim role and affirm my power. The instant I
ask for help, Life rushes to my assistance. I am safe.

I am grateful for Life's generosity. I am blessed.

Three

I can see any situation clearly and find a solution.

I do not have to work so hard to get what I want.

Every day, I am moving toward my goals.

I am in control of my own life.

My life is full of opportunities that come easily to me.

I practice forgiveness every day.

I am inspired to discover new visions for my life.

There is no right or wrong; I move beyond judgment.

Being organized and efficient allows me to be spontaneous.

I surround myself with plants, trees, and other beautiful blessings of nature.

Making decisions is easy for me, and I follow through with what I say.

I keep my mind active and alive by exploring new frontiers. Learning keeps me mentally strong.

I forgive everyone, including myself.

I am willing to see how and where I need to change.

I donate a portion of my time to helping others because I want to make the world a better place.

I release the need to blame anyone, including myself.

I am a leader. I try out new ideas, and I do what I want to do.

Today is a new day. I am in charge of all aspects of my life.

I honor and respect all the elders in my life.

I do my best to make life better for everyone in the world.

Four

I am flexible enough to change my plans if necessary.

I am grateful for the mentors in my life. I learn so much from others.

I am constantly moving forward in the direction of my goals.

I can easily see what has gone wrong and come up with a clear solution.

I am focused and direct when I need to be.

Releasing the need to be judgmental frees my life.

I make my own choices in life. No one else gets to choose for me.

I see potential everywhere. I can use my mind any way I choose.

Today I move freely and easily, knowing that each moment is new and special.

I speak up clearly and state my purpose. I love the sound of my voice.

I feel stronger simply by spending time in nature.

Whatever I choose to do, I do with care and consideration.

Today I can do whatever I put my mind to.

I view all experiences as opportunities to learn and grow.

I make positive changes easily and effortlessly.

I make wise decisions, and everything works out for the best.

I accept myself and know that I am headed in the right direction.

The work I do results in making life better for everyone.

This is a great day to create, imagine, produce, and visualize.

Everything happens in the perfect time-space sequence.

Five

I have a community who loves and appreciates me.

I always give 100 percent, and it is greatly appreciated.

I am in a harmonious relationship with life.

All areas of my life are abundant and fulfilling.

I do something special for my partner today, and that makes both of us happy.

I love my thoughts. My thoughts are my best friends.

Life consistently supplies all my needs in great abundance.

I share kind, loving thoughts with everyone in my world.

I am open and receptive to meeting new and interesting people.

I release all guilt and emotional hurt. I am free.

I am totally and completely supported by Life.

I am in harmony with all of my family.

I see harmony and healing among all people everywhere.

My life is fulfilling and satisfying.

My home is a happy place to be. I bless everyone who enters, myself included.

Today I bless with love every mouthful of food I eat.

Patience is being at peace with the process of life.

Today I thank everyone I meet for something.

Life is here for me to enjoy.

Today I am calm, centered, and balanced.

Six

I have achieved things I can feel proud of.

I retain a sense of reverence in my daily life.

I remember to breathe deeply each day.

I have an easy rhythm to my daily life.

I will always have more than enough for what I need.

I am so grateful for all that I have.

The only thing I have control of is my current thinking. This thought that I am thinking now is totally under my control.

Spiritual growth comes in ways I do not expect, so I regularly sweep out negative thoughts to clear the way for the new.

I am part of the Universe; therefore, I know there is an order, rhythm, and purpose to my life.

I release the need to criticize or judge others and myself.

I am doing the best I can with the understanding, knowledge, awareness that I have.

I rise above all limitations. I am divinely guided and inspired.

Other people respect me because I respect myself.

I am willing to move out of my comfort zone and experience life in a new way.

I respect my boundaries. I insist that others respect them, too.

The point of power is in the present moment.

Yesterday is the past. I turn my total attention to the present moment.

To let go is not to regret the past but to live and grow for the future.

I am willing to release the need to be right.

I am so pleased with where I am and proud of my accomplishments.

Seven

I find beauty wherever I look.

People love me when I am myself.

I am worthy of a very good income. It comes easily to me.

I appreciate all that I have and all that I am.

I am always refining what I say and do, and my life runs smoothly.

I now let go of old patterns, and I am willing to love myself as I am.

I am good enough just as I am, and I always have as much as I need.

The world is a work of art, and so am I.

I am a clear thinker and express myself with ease.

I am truly safe no matter what. I can face anything.

My burdens are light—like feathers in the wind.

My home and office are sacred havens. I treat my environment with respect and love.

I am grateful to others for the kindness they show me. I am filled with praise and gratitude.

My day begins and ends with gratitude.

I rejoice in each passing year of my life.

The money that comes to me today is a pleasure to handle.

I release whatever I am not using, and polish to a high gloss the things that give me joy.

The struggling is over. Whenever I need help, I ask.

I give thanks for this perfect day.

At the end of the day, I am aware that I will never live this particular day again. I am grateful to be alive.

Eight

I accept myself as someone who is supported by everyone and everything around me.

Loving others is easy when I love and accept myself.

My family and I express joyful and abundant health.

Life is bringing me everything I need and more.

I choose to think thoughts that make me feel good.

I bless my home with love and put love in every corner.

I can always find harmonious solutions to my problems.

I am kind and generous to others, and they are kind and generous to me.

I enjoy taking responsibility. I know there is something I can do to change my life.

I have the ideal neighbors. They are warmhearted and supportive.

I now take my power back. I do not have to please anyone. I am safe.

It is okay to be my own best friend. Every day I do something kind for myself.

It is with joy that I digest the experiences of my life. Life agrees with me.

I support myself in big and little ways. I do not have to please anyone. I am worthy of a fulfilling, substantial life.

I have friends I can talk to, and I feel safe with my friends.

I create new and wonderful relationships. Instead of isolating myself, I choose to open up and let the love in.

I am a willing receiver of all the good Life is bringing me.

I am my best friend. Other friends may come and go, but I am always here for me.

Life gets lighter and brighter the more I genuinely care about myself.

I bless and thank my family for nurturing me.

Nine

I love to make others feel good about themselves.

I find things to delight in every day.

I feel beautiful and lovable.

My heart is open but wise.

If someone does not like me, I do not take it personally.

I have fun with whatever I do.

My life can expand and grow and be as big and glorious
as I want it to be.

I choose healthy stimulation. I speak positively with others
and listen with compassion.

My goal in life is to be in love with every moment. I choose to
have fun doing this. I choose to be free.

Today I feel the excitement and thrill of being alive.

I allow other people to love me and see my greatness.
I now discover how wonderful I am.

Success comes to me when I give love to everyone.

I fill each day with joy and laughter.

It is okay to be sad sometimes. Sadness is just another feeling.
I allow it to be, and then it passes away.

Today my love shines out from my heart and touches
everyone I see.

This day is full of miracles.

Deep at the center of my being is an infinite well of love.

I beam kind thoughts to everyone I meet today.

I laugh at myself and at life, and nothing can touch me.

I am having one joyous experience after another.

⌒

Now that you've explored the hidden symmetry of your true
nature, we'll look at the patterns that affect you as you journey
through time. In Part II, you'll learn how your life has different
cycles and seasons just as in the natural world, and how you can
align with them.

HOW TIME AFFECTS WHERE YOU ARE

*"You are looking from the place
you are looking for."*

— AUTHOR UNKNOWN

CHAPTER 10

Your Ten
Decades and
Four Gates

Our journey through life seems pretty haphazard. Things appear to happen as a result of our own efforts, as a consequence of random events, or because of what we view as good or bad luck. But there is an invisible symmetry to life as well, a rhythm of cycles that we all predictably move through; and in each phase of time, our attention will naturally be focused in a certain direction. Each stage of life is designed to guide us, to help us make further progress in our own personal evolution.

When you discover where you are in these cycles, you can understand why you're feeling the way you are and how your experiences during this period fall into a specific pattern. Each stretch of time gives you certain homework, too; if you do the work assigned for that phase, you make the most progress. Then the next stage of life builds on that to be even more positive and powerful.

Having this information allows you to finally be in the right place at the right time, to go with the flow of your specific journey rather than fight the current. And it's never too late to align with these patterns. As you read this chapter, if you find that in some stages you were headed in the wrong direction, you can trust that the lessons will reappear again for an opportunity to get back on the right path. After all, life loves you and wants you to succeed.

We'll start out by examining the rhythm of the decades. Each is associated with one or more of the Nine Star Ki numbers, but in this case, it's not important to define them that way. Instead we can simply focus on the theme of each phase.

While each decade is important, there are certain periods within them that are more significant. For one thing, each threshold you cross as you move from one ten-year stage to the next is considered to be a powerful turning point—for instance, stepping from age 29 to 30. But there are four of these transitions that are especially critical. The Chinese call them the Four Gates, and they occur as you turn 40, 50, 60, and 70. When you pass through each of these gates, you may experience a significant break with the past, so we'll look especially closely at the meanings of these periods as we explore those decades.

In each decade, it's almost as if you're compelled to turn your attention in a new direction and to deal with issues associated with that particular stage of development. You think life is just happening to you, but in fact there is a recognizable pattern. If you're aware of it, you can make the most progress with the lessons being sent your way.

Please note that childhood is the only time period that's not split exactly into decades. Instead, the first stage is considered to last until approximately the age of 10, and the second ends at age 18.

Your Childhood: Birth to Age 10

Each child is a link in the chain of existence from the family's past to its future. When you're born, and for some time after, you maintain a connection to that mysterious land of the ancestors where you lived before you emerged into your parents' arms. In your first ten years of life, you process this enormous transition. While it's a period infused with many feelings including joy and wonder, there is also always a return to fear as you learn to trust this new body you're in, this foreign environment, and these strangers around you.

And that's the homework for this stage: with the help of your family, to work through layers of fear over the years till you reach a plateau beginning at around age ten. At this point you feel you have things pretty well figured out; it's a phase of time when you believe that you objectively understand the world and have a handle on things . . . and then the hormones kick in.

Your Childhood: Ages 11 to 18

In this era, you're soon swept away by a riptide of hormones that thrust you back deep into your emotional nature, and any sense of the logic of life disappears. No longer grounded, you're at the mercy of your feelings. The journey here is not to resist but to swim deeper into yourself while still being able to come up for air.

Your second stage is touched by fear, but it's also built upon the foundation of the first decade. If you successfully developed trust in life in the first part of childhood, then you'll be able to navigate this period relatively well. But if your early years were traumatic, this age can bring some chaos, and it can be a struggle to stay afloat. If that's the case, this phase is fraught with opportunities for difficult experiences instead of positive adventures; and it's an important time for parents, family members, and the community to step up to lend support.

Your 20s

This period actually begins around age 18 and lasts through the decade of your 20s. It's a time of adventure, when you leave home and enter life without the buffer of family to protect you. This is a time when you know one thing for sure: Your parents are idiots, and you know everything.

Watch out, world, here you come! This is often the time you'll first live on your own, have significant relationships, and obtain your first grown-up job. It's a stage of risk-taking, discovery, and surprises; and the powerful lessons you learn now can benefit you for the rest of your life.

The focus for this period is external and not so much to do with your inner emotional growth, as you venture out to learn how to function in the world. As you do, you'll be challenged repeatedly—often in positive ways—until you reach a point in the last two to three years of your 20s when you finally begin to develop a new vision for your life, a point of individuation as a maturing adult rooted in the knowledge you've gained so far. Each step of life builds on skills learned in the previous time period, and the quality of the transition here is based on how strong a sense of personal identity you've been able to develop. By your late 20s, you feel in some way that you've become truly involved with the world . . . and then the tide turns.

Your 30s

The Chinese call this a yin time, when you go within, as opposed to the 20s, which was a yang period and more focused on the outer world. When you're in your 30s, you work on emotionally integrating everything that's happened to you up till now. A lot will be churning inside and sometimes you can feel all alone with that invisible struggle. After all, this is the first time in your life that you've had to swim in your inner emotional realm without your parents by your side, so there can be difficult stretches during this decade. It's not so much about what happens *to* you at this point but about what's going on *within* you.

This decade is really the next stage of your independence, a journey of soul-searching as you grow into a deeper and wiser version of yourself. During this stage it's best not to bottle this up inside but instead to find safe places and people to express what's going on for you as a way of gaining further understanding and development. (When they're in their 30s, people often work with therapists or coaches for the first time as they try to process their experience, and it can be very helpful to do so.) Then in the last few years of this decade, a new siren song begins to be heard, and your attention is irresistibly drawn in a new direction: authenticity.

Your 40s

The 40s are another yang time, when your attention is again focused outward. Because of this, it's common to have career success, either for the first time or else at a higher level of achievement than before. You'll feel clearer, have a better sense of the big picture, and begin to develop a new idea of where to go from here.

But as you turn 40, you pass through the first of the Four Gates, those significant turning points, and often major life changes happen here—such as divorce, a career change, or a big move. This isn't coincidental. As you enter this decade, you naturally feel compelled to live more authentically. You can no longer deprive yourself of being who you are just to keep your marriage intact, earn that salary, or (you fill in the blank).

You have to stop pretending to be the person you have been. It's time to finally stand more in your power. You may feel driven to find work that's more meaningful and relationships that resonate better with who you really are. As you approach your 40s, if you've been living in a way that's not true to your inner spirit, life will conspire to make you feel so uncomfortable that you just have to make a change. It can feel as though you're being forced through a keyhole, so it's helpful to understand that this is a genuine turning point and worth all the effort!

In the Chinese view, you can live off the life force you were born with until you turn 40, but at that point you have to get real and start taking your life seriously. As you turn 40, every cell in your body calls out for change. You almost have no choice but to do what's necessary to make that transition, to create a life that's more true to who you really are. And as you end this stage, you look around to evaluate things yet again, but through a different lens: fulfillment.

Your 50s

As you approach your 50s, there can be a growing sense of *This is not what I asked for!* To one degree or another, you look around with dissatisfaction, remembering all the things you'd hoped you would have received by this stage but haven't. Or you might notice how hard you've been working but with little time to really enjoy your life.

This is another yin phase, where your focus turns inward again for the next stage of emotional maturation, and life will rub your face in all the ways that you're not happy. One pressing question that comes up in this stage stems from not feeling nourished—by your partner, by your job, and most of all by yourself. By the time you reach your 50s, you may have gotten so caught up in the demands of life—in taking care of family, career, and everyday, nose-to-the-grindstone activities—that you're taking little time for good self-care. It may even be that by the time you move into your 50s, you've developed more and more of an unhappy mind-set, getting stuck in disappointment about how things have turned out and having negative expectations of what life will bring you from here.

You've just passed through the second Gate, of course, and 50 can bring what feels like an emotional downturn. This period could very well bring up feelings of anguish about how you wanted more in life, and anger about your current circumstances may arise as well. By this stage, many women have fallen into a pattern of over-giving and under-receiving in some way. Perhaps this stems from years of taking care of a spouse or family; supporting a boss, staff, and clients; or (for most women) all of the above. Now you know in your bones that this situation of having to take care of everyone else but you has got to stop.

The same thing happens for men but in a slightly different way. They can wake up as they enter their 50s and feel like they've just spent the last 30 years at the office. Perhaps it seems as though they missed seeing their children grow up, they no longer enjoy their job, their relationship with their partner may now be more like roommates, or they have few real friends. Again, it often feels like all of the above, with so many responsibilities that they're prevented from enjoying life.

The cure for this dilemma for both men and women is to develop a healthy selfishness, where they begin to give themselves what they need. For some people, that means quitting their job and starting the business they've always dreamed of, while for others it's about healing their relationship. It can also just mean more time off to enjoy the life they've created so far.

The more you can bring the ratio of giving and receiving back into balance, the more you'll enjoy what's coming in your 60s: revitalization.

Your 60s

In Chinese culture, turning 60 is the single most important birthday of your life, considered to be the completion of one full life cycle, when you are now freed of old responsibilities. It's believed that this age is the beginning of an entirely new phase where you feel revitalized and can move forward with a new purpose. It's another yang stage when your energy goes outward again to take new action in the world. There's a sense of renewed vigor and delight in life that in previous generations in Western culture was often the result of moving into retirement and freedom from the daily grind.

In current times, of course, fewer of us are leaving our careers in this decade—but the theme of new energy and freedom is still at the forefront of the experience in the 60s. There will be an irresistible desire to have more independence, to not be so burdened by the restrictions of normal life.

The level of vitality you feel at this stage will directly correlate to the amount of willpower you've had to use up until this point in your life. We all are born with a deep reservoir of pure will, which is available for us to tap into during challenging times, using it to push through when life gets hard and there's no choice but to keep going.

However, most of us use this will too often and incorrectly, draining it as we charge through everyday life, trying to *make* things happen—to force, rather than to allow—and that depletes the supply we were meant to draw from in our 60s. But we always have the chance to replenish, to refill the reservoir of will.

One way you can do this is to allow yourself what you might call downtime, which is really about rejuvenation and deep rest— for example, a long soak in the tub or time spent in meditation or daydreaming. But on a deeper level, this is about remembering to trust the process, to understand that attempting to force your will on life only drains your energy and can block wonderful things that are trying to come to you, if you'll just stop and allow.

The age of 60 is the third Gate, where because of all the personal work you did in your 50s, you're now really moving into a new way of being in the world. One theme here has to do with creativity/fertility. As you reach 60, it's the end of an era, a turning point where your creative juices need to flow in new and different ways than before.

Usually until your early 50s, a portion of your system's attention is on your physical fertility, creating offspring to continue the family line. Whether or not you actually had children, some part of your essence was attending to this possibility. The rest of the decade phases that out, though; now as you turn 60, you're freed to express your creative urges with new adventures and ideas, exploring and making new discoveries about yourself and the world. You may travel or develop your artistic abilities or simply enjoy a more creative lifestyle overall. Interestingly, studies of creativity show that more new ideas are produced during an artist's 60s and 70s than in their 20s.

And with this renewed vitality comes a need to more deeply integrate spirituality into your identity, whether that's being part of a church community or living a more spiritual life overall. This focus prepares you for the work of the next decade: a new vision.

Your 70s

As you enter your 70s, your attention turns to refining the vision for your life, including working through any unresolved issues or old conflicts and examining what you can let go of in order to move into the future unencumbered.

As you pass through the last of your Four Gates, it's time to gain more clarity about the past and get new insights on how to release any lingering pain that still needs your attention. Sometimes this concerns relationships from years gone by. Even if the person is no longer living, it will be important for you to come to some resolution about the relationship and what went wrong, to work through a process to heal what you can for yourself. In this period of life, it's easier for you to have a wise view of what happened and why.

In Chinese culture, it's believed that your work at the age of 70 is to purify your mind, to free yourself of negative thoughts and any regrets about the past. It's a time to reflect back on your life, to let go of any remorse or sadness and instead feel a growing sense of the integrity and harmony of your journey.

As part of this process, you'll begin to detach from the everyday world, not with feelings of loss but with pride and satisfaction in who you've become. This new way of being opens you to a new life in your 80s: joy.

Your 80s

There are no more Gates to fuss with—you're free to just enjoy! Building on the work you did in your 70s, the momentum of life is directing your energy inward to cultivate the "sage heart," a state of pure wisdom, peace, and joy.

In this decade, you could be brought to a second stage of letting go, where at some point you might need to release your attachment to some of your material possessions and move from what you called home to a smaller space. You may need to accept that your physical vitality is diminished and that there are limitations on what you can do. If you resist and hold tightly to what you think your life has to look like, you won't be able to find the joy that's waiting for you in this phase.

There's a term in Chinese culture for an elderly person who's staying overly attached to the past: a ghost. Just like a ghost is trapped in a space they don't realize is no longer theirs, if you're locked into thinking that you have to retain every aspect of your old life, you can never relax into the beauty of this stage of conscious aging and experience your joy. If you stay in harmony as your physical energy fades, you can effortlessly move into the next decade with appreciation.

Your 90s

At this stage there will be a growing ethereal awareness as your physical energy continues to become delicate, and you balance between Earth and heaven. The work in this decade will be to become more and more present, with a developing appreciation of the preciousness of each moment. Watch in awe as the beams of morning sunlight glow in the leaves outside your window, relish the feel of the breeze on your skin, and soak in every second of the pure delight of watching your great-grandchild at play.

You don't feel afraid when you see the trees lose their leaves in autumn, or as the cold slows things down in winter. You know these are natural events, and just as you can find pleasure and beauty in those seasons, you can find the same in this phase of life. Use your understanding of nature as your guiding principle, and this can be a time of ease and delight.

Age 100+

If you reach the century mark and beyond, the Chinese believe you emerge into what's like a second childhood. However, this time it's not immersed in fear but in wisdom. Every moment of fear that you've transcended through courage, every lesson you've learned, every moment of love you've felt brings you to this point of wisdom, nonattachment, and total flow. Good job!

Now that we've seen the meanings and messages of the decades in life, in the next chapter we turn to focus on shorter time periods. Each individual year also has an energetic signature that affects both your inner and outer worlds.

CHAPTER 11

YOUR PERSONAL
SEASONS

Each year has a theme that's represented by one of the nine numbers, and it will bring you certain experiences from the outside world as well as stimulate thoughts and feelings in your inner world that are in alignment with that pattern. If you're aware of the year's design and direction, you won't feel bewildered or blame yourself for what's occurring—it can be such an incredible relief to know why things are going the way they are. This lets you have realistic expectations for your experience and helps you make the most progress during the year, rather than groping in the dark.

The annual change in energy doesn't happen on your birthday; instead, the timing has more to do with the calendar year. But it's also not the case that on January 1, the theme of the new year abruptly drops into place in your life. It's more gradual than that, and I often notice a two- to three-month threshold that people cross from year to year.

In Nine Star Ki, the "official" New Year's Day is actually February 4, but I usually don't pay much attention to that specific date. Instead, what I observe is that toward the end of any particular year, usually around November or December, the influence of the current phase starts to wear off and the energy of the coming year begins to flood in. In fact, in late fall or early winter, it's common to notice new developments or changes, or even just shifts in how you're thinking or feeling. If you don't notice anything in that time frame, then by January or early February, it will be obvious that things are definitely different!

Pay attention this year to what happens from November to January and see if you notice the shift.

For each year, there's a way to go with the flow rather than fight the current—and as you align yourself to the direction the year is taking you, life can unfold almost effortlessly. As you read the descriptions in this chapter, find the year you're currently in so that you can start to apply these insights about how to live in the rhythm of the time. You can also look at the information about previous years to see how the meaning applies in the context of your past experience.

Important note: You don't begin to be influenced by these yearly cycles until you reach the age of 18 (or in rare cases when you leave home and are completely independent prior to that time). If you're under 18, you should look at where your parents are in any particular year. Because you're under their influence, what's affecting them will impact you directly as well.

Under each yearly category, I'll list the most recent year you were under that influence and then the one coming up next. It can be fascinating to look back to see what year you were in when you had a breakup, got married, or made a big move, in order to understand why that experience happened the way it did, based on the theme of the year.

When we look at where you are in the cycles of the individual years of your life, we use only your first number; the other two numbers don't matter here. So for instance, if you're a 1.4.2, you'll look at the dates following "If your first number is One."

Because this is a nine-year cycle, you can track the past or future simply by adding or subtracting nine years. For example, if 2013 is a Seven year for you, 2022 would be your next Seven year (nine years later), and 2004 was your previous Seven year (nine years in the past). There's also a chart at the end of this chapter to let you track your journey through more years in your past and future.

One Year: Dream the Dream

If your first number is One:
2013, 2022

If your first number is Two:
2012, 2021

If your first number is Three:
2011, 2020

If your first number is Four:
2010, 2019

If your first number is Five:
2009, 2018

If your first number is Six:
2008, 2017

If your first number is Seven:
2007, 2016

If your first number is Eight:
2006, 2015

If your first number is Nine:
2005, 2014

This is the first year in a brand-new era for you, so it's an important time of new beginnings. However, it's not what you might expect—it's not a big launch into a whirlwind of activity. Instead, it's a time when your system needs to reboot.

In the cycles of nature, the One year is associated with the energy of winter. In most climates, when you look outside in this season, it appears that nothing's alive or growing. It seems pretty desolate. But in fact, we know that's not true. Deep down in the ground, the seeds are soaking in all the rich nutrients in that cold, wet soil; and we know that if they stay there all winter, what sprouts in the spring will be able to grow to its fullest potential. We'd never dream of running into the garden in the middle of winter, pulling the seeds up out of the ground, and shouting, "C'mon, c'mon, c'mon, grow!"

So you need to apply this awareness to your One year as well. It's not a time to take action. Instead, it's a time to go inward, rest, replenish your energy, and dream about what you'd love from life in this next stage. In nature, winter is a time of hibernation, and your experience this year will reflect that. You may find that you feel like staying home more and being quiet, and this is because your system needs to slow down and turn inward; the work for this year is internal.

If a client comes to me for a reading about a new business they're about to launch and I see that they're in their One year, I know that even if it's the best idea since the beginning of time—even if they have a great business plan, tons of investors, Super Bowl commercials booked, and a toll-free number with operators standing by—if they launch the business this year, the phones will hardly ring. And then they may scratch their heads, shrug their shoulders, and think, *Well, I guess it wasn't such a great idea after all,* and give up.

It may indeed have been a fantastic idea, but the timing was wrong. There are certain years that support getting a new business out there, but this isn't one of them. If you do have to launch something in your One year, it won't be the end of the world, but you should expect slow growth, not immediate results.

There *are* things you're supposed to do in your One year, and the most important of all is to dream where you want to go from here. Give yourself time to space out, float, daydream, and fantasize about what your life could be—and don't hold back! Get creative and allow yourself infinite possibilities in your fantasies. This isn't the time to figure out *how* to make your dreams come true or to create a practical action plan. Don't be scared that you'll end up behaving carelessly. If you imagine quitting your job, leaving your family, and running off to Spain to become a flamenco dancer, your common sense will click in at the next stage of the cycle. But if you don't allow yourself your wildest dreams now, if you try to create a logical plan instead, you'll significantly limit your future growth, just as if you pulled the seeds out of the ground in the winter.

The energy of a One year has to do with feelings rather than facts. So it's best not to have CNN or radio talk shows on in the background all day. Allow silence or listen to music. Watch fewer news shows and documentaries in favor of fanciful movies; read less nonfiction and more fiction. A One year is also a great time to learn, study, or do any creative activities. If you travel, it's best to

go for pure relaxation or an adventure rather than a tightly scheduled business trip.

There are challenges that can come up in each of the nine years, and for the One year, there's a possibility of financial or health concerns, usually to a very minor degree but sometimes dramatic. These stimulate and intertwine with the emotional patterns for the year, which center around fear. You're more inclined to get caught up in fear about whatever emerges this year, and it's good to remember that these feelings can have nothing to do with the reality of the situation but are more to do with your being swept away into frightened fantasies about what *could* happen. Talk to friends for reassurance and a reality check.

Above all, it's so helpful to remind yourself that in a year like this, things are happening behind the scenes that aren't yet visible. If you rest on that certainty, you can know that you're quietly creating a powerful future.

Two Year: Build the Foundation

If your first number is One:
2005, 2014

If your first number is Two:
2013, 2022

If your first number is Three:
2012, 2021

If your first number is Four:
2011, 2020

If your first number is Five:
2010, 2019

If your first number is Six:
2009, 2018

If your first number is Seven:
2008, 2017

If your first number is Eight:
2007, 2016

If your first number is Nine:
2006, 2015

After using the One year to imagine what this new era could be, the Two year is the time to start to build the foundation for where you want to go from here. The theme of this year has to do with the essence of Mother. A stereotypical mom has to plan well to accomplish all she has to do in any particular day. She has to get the kids ready for school and then head to work in time for a slew of meetings, complete the project on schedule, pick up the dry cleaning, and chauffeur the kids to various after-school activities while still getting dinner on the table in time. If she thinks ahead and stays organized, she can get everything done successfully.

So in your Two year, it's time to get your ducks in a row. Similar to a mother at the beginning of her day, there's a lot of activity coming to your life next year, so if you plan ahead and make sure things are in order, you'll do fine. You can now figure out what's needed to support the dream you created the previous year. If you're going to start a new business, for example, this would be the time to work on the business plan, get your board of advisors and investors, figure out the logistics, and cover all the details. It's a time to talk to others as well, to get solid advice and to ground your ideas.

A Two year is also about helpers showing up. You may find that new friends just drop into your lap or that you easily find the professionals who can assist you in your plan. It's a great time to network, going to events or workshops that help you develop whatever it is you're wanting to start. Take every opportunity you can to connect with people, whether it's coffee with old or new friends or participating in an online forum. Tell your story, share ideas, and stay as receptive as possible to help or advice others offer you.

Note that at the beginning of a Two year, it's possible to miss some opportunities because you don't notice that the energy has shifted and helpers are appearing. Here's what happens: By the time you reach the last stages of your One year, you're accustomed to the fact that life has slowed down considerably, and it's possible that you may feel quite solitary, even cut off from others. Not knowing that this is a pattern that lasts for just one year, it's likely that on some level, you now believe this is how life will be! You've had so many months of experiencing this reality, and you have no reason to think it's going to end.

So as your Two year begins to show up, you could miss the fact that the scenery around you is starting to change. Instead, you're walking down the road with blinders on, repeating this old One-year story to yourself. You might not notice that there are friendly folks standing on the sidelines, offering their hands and trying to get your attention: "Uh, can I help you?" So in the late fall and early winter of your One year, you should be watching for those first opportunities to flow in from the influence of the Two year and allow support to enter your life.

An issue that will come up in a Two year centers around home. You may suddenly want to change things at home, whether that's rearranging furniture, remodeling, or planning to move. It's better not to do an actual move this year, but instead wait till the following year; however, this year is a good time to make all the plans and preparations.

Relationship issues may surface as well. It's not unusual to feel unsatisfied in one or more relationships this year—in fact, it's a great time to think about what will make you truly feel loved and nurtured and how things can be brought more into balance in that regard. At the same time, it's important to pay attention to your own responsibility for creating or contributing to the situation and not lay all the blame on the other person. As part of this theme, family issues may be at the forefront this year and you could be called upon to help in some way, or be forced to work through problems, especially with your mother or female relatives.

There's a possibility of dropping into victim mode this year, feeling sorry for yourself or upset that people are taking advantage of you. To counteract this, be sure to practice good self-care, be mindful of boundaries, and take time to enjoy the pleasures of life as it is right now.

Things will still tend to feel a little slow in your Two year, so you'll have to practice patience. It's not quite time to take action, so stay focused on thinking things through and completing your plans, building the foundation you're about to launch from!

Three Year: Go for It

If your first number is One: 2006, 2015	If your first number is Six: 2010, 2019
If your first number is Two: 2005, 2014	If your first number is Seven: 2009, 2018
If your first number is Three: 2013, 2022	If your first number is Eight: 2008, 2017
If your first number is Four: 2012, 2021	If your first number is Nine: 2007, 2016
If your first number is Five: 2011, 2020	

If you've been wanting to start a business, make a change, initiate a project, or begin anything important, now is the time to go for it! The Three year is like the full force of spring, when plants break through the ground and there's a natural sense of forward movement overall. Whatever you start in a Three year can have a big response from the world because this is your time of growth and change.

The influence of this year actually begins to trickle in during the late fall or early winter of your Two year, and that's when you can suddenly begin to feel twitchy. You'll start thinking, *I've just got to make a change!* You may want to quit your job, leave your relationship, or move somewhere new. In fact, what's happening is that your system is feeling the change coming but slightly misinterpreting the information, thinking that you're the one who has to make the shift happen. The fact is that you could hide in the closet with a blanket over your head in a Three year, and change will still find you!

In the spring, we have a natural sense of hope and optimism. The days are getting longer, the leaves are sprouting, and there's a sense of new possibilities; likewise, in your Three year, you'll likely feel your optimism returning after two years when you

might have been unsure at times if things were ever going to get moving again. But it's important not to get swept away in your enthusiasm and be careless. A Three year can be a time of rapid progress, but you may feel such a sense of urgency that you go too fast and overlook some important part of your plan.

Along with feelings of optimism come frustration and impatience, increasing the possibility that you can act impulsively. At the extreme range of these feelings is anger, where you might lash out at others. Even if this isn't your nature, you may become more easily upset or irritated in a Three year; the more you can be aware of this possibility, the more quickly you can catch yourself before it causes problems.

Another way you can ride the energy of the year is to stay physically active. This has the double benefit of aligning with its theme of forward movement along with giving you a way to burn off any of the frustration or stress that can surface at this time. Even if you're not usually the type to exercise regularly, this is the perfect year to focus on ways to move your body!

When a plant sprouts in the spring, there's a plan built into its DNA so that it grows in a deliberate way to achieve its fullest potential. Similarly, it's important to focus on your action plan this year. Now that things are moving along, you need to keep up with developments and adapt as situations change. This means staying organized and active, and on a regular basis reevaluating the structure you've built for whatever you're doing. If things aren't going as you thought they would, it's time to rethink and adjust the plan to accommodate the new circumstances.

Your vision of the future is an important theme for this period. It's essential that you ask yourself what it is you really want for the next few years. Sometimes in a Three year, you can get too shortsighted, too focused on the immediate goal, without seeing where it's really taking you. Devote some time to think about what the life you want looks like—literally. You might create a vision board with pictures cut out of magazines that represent your goals for the future or write a list or description of things you want in your life. But the essential final step is to let go of any attachment to how they need to show up. The more you focus on a specific outcome, the less chance there is that you'll achieve the even more wonderful results that life can give you.

Four Year: Ride the Wind

If your first number is One:
2007, 2016

If your first number is Two:
2006, 2015

If your first number is Three:
2005, 2014

If your first number is Four:
2013, 2022

If your first number is Five:
2012, 2021

If your first number is Six:
2011, 2020

If your first number is Seven:
2010, 2019

If your first number is Eight:
2009, 2018

If your first number is Nine:
2008, 2017

This is the second half of a two-year cycle of change that began with your Three year, but it has a different flavor than the first half. It's as if change has sped up, so things seem less predictable. The direction you thought you were going can suddenly change or circumstances intervene so that you're now not sure what's going to happen. There are distractions and new developments that can make you feel indecisive and unsure; there seem to be so many options, and it's hard to know which one to choose.

The most common comment I hear from people in a Four year is: "Everything feels so up in the air!" In fact, the image for the Four *is* the wind; and the theme of this year is about learning to ride that wind, accepting that you feel uncertain about how everything is going to work out. At times, it may feel like the rug has been pulled out from under you, and it can be so helpful to recognize that this is the pattern for the year, not due to some mistake you've made. When you can avoid blaming yourself for

what's going on, you'll be able to see that wonderful things are happening in the midst of all this change!

It's true that the energy of a Four year stimulates more indecisiveness within you, so you may waver or back off from a decision or get distracted by all the possible choices. The general advice for this time is to expect change but to try to stay focused on whatever it was that you started the year before. You may have to adjust that vision this year, but it's best not to change horses midstream.

Feelings of frustration or impatience can come up more easily, and it's important to recognize them as part of the year's influence rather than take them too seriously or base decisions on these repeating patterns of emotion. A Four year can incline you to behave impulsively; alternatively, you may take too much of a "wait and see" attitude and let opportunities pass you by. It's important to keep moving, but to stay grounded by seeking common-sense advice as you go.

If a relationship is nearing the end of its life span, it's not uncommon for the decision to end it to be made in your Four year and the actual "divorce" to take effect the following year. It may be a decision about ending a marriage, or some other kind of parting of ways from someone you've been connected to. The thought process around this situation will contribute to your feelings of uncertainty, of course, and it can help to remember that the turbulence you're experiencing is a natural part of the design for the year and won't last.

The theme of influence is very strong in a Four year, and this can mean that now you show up as an influential person with friends and in your career. But it can also mean that you're more easily influenced by others' opinions, and they may make you feel uncertain about your own. You might make a decision, and then your best friend says, "Are you *kidding?*" and you'll back off to rethink things. So while it's helpful to bounce things off advisors this year, be discerning about whom you choose to listen to.

Keep in mind that a very beneficial aspect of this theme can also affect you now, as someone of great influence might show up in your life. The Chinese would call this person an Elder, which they define as someone who's in a superior position to you in life such as a boss, a mentor, a teacher, or an older family member. This year, it may be that someone higher up in your profession takes on the role of a mentor for you, or someone of power and influence helps you go to the next level in your career or life overall.

It's not that you have to go out and find this person, as the energy of the year will just naturally support their appearing in your life. But you do need to be able to recognize what's going on and say yes to the opportunity. Of course, this individual probably isn't going to ring your doorbell, but life will create opportunities for you to meet them, and all you have to do is say yes at those times.

Five Year: Eye of the Hurricane

If your first number is One:
2008, 2017

If your first number is Two:
2007, 2016

If your first number is Three:
2006, 2015

If your first number is Four:
2005, 2014

If your first number is Five:
2013, 2022

If your first number is Six:
2012, 2021

If your first number is Seven:
2011, 2020

If your first number is Eight:
2010, 2019

If your first number is Nine:
2009, 2018

Fasten your seat belt—the Five year is an intense one, and it can be quite a roller-coaster ride! Wonderful opportunities may fall into your lap, and a lot happens overall. It can be a year of extremes; by the fall of your Five year, you may be ready to just go sit on the beach and watch the waves, longing to be bored for once!

The good news is that the Five year is considered a time of fulfillment, when all the hard work you've been doing for the past four years starts to produce results. You may finally feel like you're getting somewhere, aren't having to fight so hard to get noticed, and can settle in with a growing sense that you've accomplished something and can now work to deepen your results.

In fact, anything that you start in a Five year is said to be very powerful and has the potential to grow deep roots. If you partner with someone to start a business, it can be quite a significant and long-lasting collaboration. A marriage formed in a Five year can be quite a deep and strong relationship. But a Five year is called a time of both beginnings *and* endings, so while the things you start are powerful, it's also possible that something may come to a close in a powerful way as well. If a divorce is going to happen, often the decision is made during the Four year, but the official split will take effect in the Five year. It's also not uncommon for surprise divorces to happen in a Five year, when one partner suddenly says to the other, "You know I haven't been happy for a long time, and I can't take it anymore!" Yet the other person may not have been aware of how bad things had actually gotten.

The energy of the year also brings up your own issues of dissatisfaction, but this doesn't mean you're guaranteed to split with your partner! The Five year gives you the opportunity to look at your relationship and heal or improve anything that needs attention. It can be a powerful time of reconnecting.

The advice for a Five year is to try to stay as centered as you can. (Remember that the energy of the Five nature is all about the center.) Being in this stage is really like standing in the eye of a hurricane: if you make one move, you'll get swept up by those strong winds. Another way to imagine it is the way the Chinese think of it—as staring into the eyes of a dragon. If you're eyeball to eyeball with a dragon, you don't want to blink, let alone make any sudden movements!

It's best not to move house this year, but to stay put. That can sometimes be difficult, because the year may bring you opportunities that require you to move. It's best if you can make all the plans during this year, but do the actual moving the following year. If you absolutely have to move in your Five year, just make provisions for the possibility of complications that may affect you during the transition or for a while afterward, or at least allow extra time to rest and adjust after you've arrived.

Overall, the patterns of the year arrange it so you can end up at the center of things in some way. It may seem like everyone's coming to you for advice, or you're being called on to help others solve problems. Be aware that even if you're not usually the type to over-give, this year inclines you to feel too responsible for others' welfare, and you may have to watch your boundaries and mind your own good self-care. This is a wonderful time to enjoy home, family, and friends, and to soak in all the blessings you've received so far!

Six Year: Own Your Power

If your first number is One:
2009, 2018

If your first number is Two:
2008, 2017

If your first number is Three:
2007, 2016

If your first number is Four:
2006, 2015

If your first number is Five:
2005, 2014

If your first number is Six:
2013, 2022

If your first number is Seven:
2012, 2021

If your first number is Eight:
2011, 2020

If your first number is Nine:
2010, 2019

With the Six year, you enter a two-year cycle of reaping rewards. This particular year is a phase when people tend to graduate, retire, get a promotion, inherit money, or in some way feel that they're

achieving a new level in life. It's a time when you can ease up a bit. For instance, you won't have to chase clients to try to get their business as much as you used to because they'll come to you. People will give you more respect and may spread the word that you're the one to hire because of all your knowledge and experience. So the phone will ring more often, and you may end up working harder than ever, but in a different way from before.

And in this kind of year, it's very likely that you'll feel a growing sense of pride, perhaps for the first time in years. You start to see that you have indeed reached a certain level of achievement, and you feel good about that. Some of your ambitions may have been fulfilled—or at least you feel that you're standing in your power now in a way that you weren't before. It's important to let those feelings soak in. Don't judge yourself as being egotistical; right now, it's like vitamins for you to allow yourself to feel proud and more sure of yourself. It gives you the sense of power you need to make clear decisions from here.

One caution about a year like this is that you can tend to be a bit brittle in your outlook. You're more likely to see things as too black and white and miss the nuances. You can get too caught up in principles and not be able to just let things go. You may come across to other people as more critical or fussy than usual, and you'll definitely be inclined to be too self-critical. You'll certainly notice criticism from others more in this year; when that happens, try to just breathe through it and not take it personally.

In a Six year, you're naturally drawn to examine how meaningful life is, and you may suddenly find that you can no longer deprive yourself just to get by. If your job hasn't felt like it's really "you" for a while now, this may be the year when you can't stay in denial. If any of your relationships seem inauthentic, now is the time when you'll feel the need to find more people you can really be yourself with.

One essential task is to take time to reflect on your vision for your future. But this vision isn't so much what you *want* in terms of a fancy car, nice house, and loving family; instead, it's your sense of what your ideal life is meant to be, what your sacred purpose really is. The theme of the Six has to do with your connection with the Divine, however you define it. This is about the long view and the highest use of who you came here to be.

We all have a calling in life, and in a Six year, two things can happen around that theme: (1) You may feel as if you're finally moving further into your true calling; or (2) you may begin to realize that in all the fervor to achieve your goals, you've gotten caught up in the hard work and lost touch with the original inspiration that sent you in this direction in the first place. This is the year to refine your sense of what your ideal life really is. Take some time to evaluate the quality of your current lifestyle and see if it includes enough sacred space.

A Six year is an excellent time to have subtle energy work, such as acupuncture or energy clearing. Don't disregard the energy of your environments, either; a space clearing can be the best gift you give yourself this year, releasing any stuck or stagnant energy that may have invisibly built up over time. You can hire a professional to do it or devise your own personal form of clearing to make the house feel truly blessed.

Seven Year: Experience Beauty

If your first number is One:
2010, 2019

If your first number is Two:
2009, 2018

If your first number is Three:
2008, 2017

If your first number is Four:
2007, 2016

If your first number is Five:
2006, 2015

If your first number is Six:
2005, 2014

If your first number is Seven:
2013, 2022

If your first number is Eight:
2012, 2021

If your first number is Nine:
2011, 2020

In the distant past, when everyone lived off the land, the time right after the harvest had been brought in was particularly special. They'd toiled all spring to sow the seeds, tended them through the summer, and then worked hard at the end of summer to bring in the crops at the peak of their ripeness so that there would be plenty of food to last through the winter. But once all the work was done, they'd do what people do whenever they complete a big undertaking—have a party to celebrate their accomplishment!

This is that year for you. It's meant to be a time of celebration, of doing things to reward yourself for all your hard work and many achievements. In a Seven year, it's important to give yourself opportunities for pleasure. Take a vacation, buy yourself something nice, enjoy wonderful meals, and give yourself special experiences. Of course, do this within your means! If you can't afford that round-the-world cruise, then go away for a weekend. If a three-star restaurant isn't in the budget, have a beautiful meal somewhere that won't break the bank. You must find ways to give yourself rewards—in a Seven year, life usually gives you ample chances to celebrate, so you won't have to go looking for the opportunity to do so.

The theme of this year is really about experiencing beauty and appreciating the preciousness of your life. And that can be done even without spending extra money. When you serve a meal, use your good china, arrange the food beautifully on your plate, take a few moments to look at how lovely it all is, and then savor every bite. Bring a flower in from the garden and place it in a little vase on your desk before you get down to work. Look around your house to see if there are ways you can make it a lovely place for you to be. Most of all, take time each day to soak in the beauty all around you. Notice how the sun warms your skin, savor your cup of tea, breathe in the scent of a flower, and delight in all the moments of your experience.

In a Seven year, there's also a risk that you can flip into the opposite of celebration and rewards. What can happen so subtly that you hardly notice is you start worrying about finances:

Wow, the economy is still in terrible shape, and they're talking about layoffs at work. I'd better cancel my vacation this year, just in case. And I'm going to stop eating out so much—in fact, meat is so expensive now that I'm going to try to live on rice and beans. Hmm, maybe I should rent out a room in my house . . .

Instead of embracing beauty and pleasure, your energy can contract into deprivation, and that goes against the flow of the year. If you do this, you set your entire system off balance, which can affect not only what happens this year, but how future years go for you as well.

It's important to watch for ways in which your mind starts heading in the direction of making life smaller and catch yourself before you go too far down that road. Of course you shouldn't make careless choices with money, but the worst thing you could do this year is fall into stinginess.

One challenge that can happen in a Seven year is that you're suddenly given the responsibility for taking care of another person, such as an elderly parent or someone who's ailing or in difficulty in some way. Part of the pattern of energy here centers around responsibility and the fact that if it's given to you in this particular year, there's a chance that you'll let it weigh too heavily on your shoulders and not ask for help when you should.

If you find that you've been handed this kind of challenge, don't try to tough things out on your own without letting people know how hard it is for you. Find ways to share the load, delegate some of the responsibility, and make very sure the situation doesn't result in your depriving yourself.

Sometimes this is called the Year of Joy, and it can be a lovely time, when everything seems to happen with more ease, including the chance of falling in love. It doesn't mean that "bad" things can't happen, but that if they do, either they'll happen more easily than in any other year or will be easier for you to handle. No matter what this year brings, you can make the best use of it by always remembering to see the beauty around you.

Eight Year: Caterpillar in the Cocoon

If your first number is One:
2011, 2020

If your first number is Six:
2006, 2015

If your first number is Two:
2010, 2019

If your first number is Seven:
2005, 2014

If your first number is Three:
2009, 2018

If your first number is Eight:
2013, 2022

If your first number is Four:
2008, 2017

If your first number is Nine:
2012, 2021

If your first number is Five:
2007, 2016

We know that in nature, the caterpillar goes into the cocoon for the process of transforming into a butterfly. But this can't be a comfortable experience for this creature—its whole body has to break down and re-form! I often equate an Eight year to that phase in the cycles of nature when the caterpillar endures the process of breaking apart its previous identity through this powerful transformation.

For you, this year is a time when deep change begins to stir inside, but it may not be immediately apparent to you that this is what's going on. In fact, what often happens in an Eight year is that you feel like things just aren't right. As you move into the influence of this year, you can begin to think, *This is not what I ordered!* You'll be confronted by all of the ways you're not feeling satisfied or fulfilled with where you stand at this point. It may be that life arranges events to force the issue, or it may just be that these thoughts and feelings arise without much stimulation from the outside world.

This is actually a time of deep reevaluation, when you're given the opportunity to look at what's not working and what you really need in order to be happy. It can be so reassuring to understand that there's a reason for how you're feeling and that there are specific ways to navigate this year successfully. Just like the caterpillar doesn't turn into a butterfly overnight, this is a process that develops slowly for you over several months. You can't just sit down on a Sunday afternoon and figure out what to do.

This is change that begins deep inside, out of sight for quite some time as you journey through the year. If you're not aware this is happening, you can feel as though you're stuck and stagnating, but that's not the case. You can best support this process by taking time to ponder what you want to be different, but what's most important to understand is that this is a time when you just have to stew in your own juices. Surrender and trust.

If you resist, the year will be a struggle; if you let yourself get too exasperated, the temptation to take action, to blast out of this stuck place, can be strong. But that decision would be premature and wrongheaded. It'll be hard to think things through clearly, so it's best to be patient and wait to act until the following year.

At the extreme, it can seem like things are falling apart, but this usually happens when you've been going too far in the wrong direction and life is giving you a course correction. While it can be difficult to just let go, understand that there's a reason for this experience and benefits will come down the road. Remember, what's going to result from this process is a butterfly!

The image for an Eight is the mountain. In the mountain, there is a cave; and the cave is where the treasure is. That treasure is the ageless wisdom that gives you the power for deep transformation. Another way of understanding an Eight year is that it's a time to retreat into the mountain cave to engage with that alchemical process that will change your future. So if you feel like spending more time alone this year, this is the reason.

Of course if you're deep in a cave, it can be hard to communicate with the outside world, so this year there can be communication problems. For instance, you thought your ticket says the plane leaves at 3:00 but it left at 2:00. You signed the contract but didn't notice clause 18 that included that impossible deadline. In an Eight year, triple-check your travel plans and have someone else go over that contract; and if it's important information, don't

assume that someone else understood what you told them or that you got their message clearly.

An Eight year is a great opportunity to hit the pause button, go within to take quiet time to evaluate your life, and watch your feelings come up. But don't act on your frustrations—just feel them and then let them move on. Think, study, read, take classes, enjoy home and family, and know that change is slowly happening deep within.

Nine Year: Step into the Light

If your first number is One:
2012, 2021

If your first number is Two:
2011, 2020

If your first number is Three:
2010, 2019

If your first number is Four:
2009, 2018

If your first number is Five:
2008, 2017

If your first number is Six:
2007, 2016

If your first number is Seven:
2006, 2015

If your first number is Eight:
2005, 2014

If your first number is Nine:
2013, 2022

As you enter your Nine year, it can seem like the sun is coming out again, and you may feel lighter and brighter and more positive. The year before, it was probably hard to get clarity; now the skies are clearing and it's obvious that things have changed. New ideas and opportunities will start to come more easily, and you may find yourself getting excited about life again. In fact, as things really start to pop, you may have trouble keeping up! It's possible to have too many balls in the air and get so overwhelmed that nothing gets done. It's easy to feel scattered during this year, even to the point of things feeling chaotic at times.

This year may stimulate agitation or anxiety even if you aren't usually the type of person to feel that way. The energy here is like that of a hummingbird in constant motion, with wings moving so fast, they're just a blur. This can mean that it's hard for you to pay attention to any one thing for very long, or there's an undercurrent of nervousness. It can be exacerbated by the fact that sudden change could happen this year, and that can certainly be unnerving.

The Nine year is the last of the cycle, a time of completion, and your experience can be that some things come to an end. Your best friend may get transferred to a new city, or a relationship might come to a surprise end in some other way. Your career may be affected, or you could notice a series of more minor things that are coming to completion now. If you're unaware that this is the theme of the year, you *can* begin to feel anxious, as if you've been doing something to cause this to happen! Instead, understand that timing supports these events, and that everything has a life span, even relationships. As you allow one thing to end, it creates space for new opportunities in life.

Also, do look at consciously finishing whatever you can this year. That can mean completing projects you've been working on or even choosing to end a relationship or job. It's a good time to clear clutter and make new space in your home or office. But it's about completion in your inner world as well: You're about to cross the threshold into a whole new era, and you don't want to carry old baggage along with you! Look at any issues of invisible clutter that are clogging your life. Are there old habits you've been wanting to let go of? What patterns of thought or belief no longer serve you? What friends have you outgrown? Are there aspects of your lifestyle that no longer work for you? Now is the time when it'll be easier to make positive change and finish up old issues.

Things come to light in a Nine year, and that can mean you're in the spotlight or more easily noticed in some way. So it's a great time to launch that new marketing or public-relations campaign or to send out your résumé. If you're dating, this is a year when you could find a big response to your profile in online-dating

sites, or you'll get attention when you go out. It's a great year for love and romance, so take advantage of it!

This whole theme of things coming to light includes things you may not want to be seen, however. (For example, President Clinton's affair with Monica Lewinsky was revealed during one of his Nine years.) You may be pulled over for speeding for the first time in your life because you were the one to catch the police officer's attention! This is a year when life will help you clean up your act.

This isn't the time for long periods of solitude. Go to social events and classes, travel, and hang out anywhere you can be around like-minded people. This is about having fun and being in touch with your joy. Don't judge it irresponsible or a waste of time if you do something just for the fun of it—that's actually your homework for the year, so go for it!

Flowing Through the Years

Your experience in any particular year will also be affected by what your first number is. For one thing, you'll feel more comfortable in a year that matches your energy. If your first number is Eight, you may well enjoy sitting in that Eight-year cave, because that vibration is familiar to you, while someone who's a Three may feel more stuck and frustrated because it's their nature to prefer action. If you're a One, the One year has an energy that you understand, while someone who's a Nine may judge it as too slow and boring.

In the end, what's really important to know is that since you now have the awareness of what each year brings, you can allow it and move with it. The more you align with the theme of the year, the more progress you'll make and the more you'll enjoy it. You'll understand why things are happening the way they are and won't resist or judge your experience; you'll know what to pay attention to and the meaning of the lessons coming your way. When you recognize the patterns of any phase, you're empowered to be in the right place at the right time!

Chart of Your Yearly Cycles

When we look at where you are in the cycles of the individual years of your life, we use only your first number; the other two numbers don't matter here. So for instance, if you are a 7.2.1, you would look at the information under "If Your First Number Is Seven."

Some of the years that follow may be ones when you weren't past 18, or even alive yet—just ignore any of those years and use the ones that fall within your adult lifetime. If you don't see a year you're interested in below, remember this is a nine-year cycle. So for instance, if you're looking for the year 2032, you'd just count back nine years to 2023 and find where that year (2023) falls in the chart below, because both of those years will be affected by the same theme.

Reminder: You do not begin to be influenced by these yearly cycles until you reach the age of 18 (or in rare cases, when you leave home and are independent prior to that time).

If Your First Number Is One:

Your One Years Are: 2022; 2013; 2004; 1995; 1986; 1977; 1968; 1959; 1950

Your Two Years Are: 2023; 2014; 2005; 1996; 1987; 1978; 1969; 1960; 1951

Your Three Years Are: 2024; 2015; 2006; 1997; 1988; 1979; 1970; 1961; 1952

Your Four Years Are: 2025; 2016; 2007; 1998; 1989; 1980; 1971; 1962; 1953

Your Five Years Are: 2026; 2017; 2008; 1999; 1990; 1981; 1972; 1963; 1954

Your Six Years Are: 2027; 2018; 2009; 2000; 1991; 1982; 1973; 1964; 1955;

Your Seven Years Are: 2028; 2019; 2010; 2001; 1992; 1983; 1974; 1965; 1956

Your Eight Years Are: 2029; 2020; 2011; 2002; 1993; 1984; 1975; 1966; 1957

Your Nine Years Are: 2030; 2021; 2012; 2003; 1994; 1985; 1976; 1967; 1958

If Your First Number Is Two:

Your One Years Are: 2030; 2021; 2012; 2003; 1994; 1985; 1976; 1967; 1958

Your Two Years Are: 2031; 2022; 2013; 2004; 1995; 1986; 1977; 1968; 1959

Your Three Years Are: 2032; 2023; 2014; 2005; 1996; 1987; 1978; 1969; 1960

Your Four Years Are: 2024; 2015; 2006; 1997; 1988; 1979; 1970; 1961; 1952

Your Five Years Are: 2025; 2016; 2007; 1998; 1989; 1980; 1971; 1962; 1953

Your Six Years Are: 2026; 2017; 2008; 1999; 1990; 1981; 1972; 1963; 1954

Your Seven Years Are: 2027; 2018; 2009; 2000; 1991; 1982; 1973; 1964; 1955

Your Eight Years Are: 2028; 2019; 2010; 2001; 1992; 1983; 1974; 1965; 1956

Your Nine Years Are: 2029; 2020; 2011; 2002; 1993; 1984; 1975; 1966; 1957

If Your First Number Is Three:

Your One Years Are: 2029; 2020; 2011; 2002; 1993; 1984; 1975; 1966; 1957

Your Two Years Are: 2030; 2021; 2012; 2003; 1994; 1985; 1976; 1967; 1958

Your Three Years Are: 2031; 2022; 2013; 2004; 1995; 1986; 1977; 1968; 1959

Your Four Years Are: 2023; 2014; 2005; 1996; 1987; 1978; 1969; 1960; 1951

Your Five Years Are: 2024; 2015; 2006; 1997; 1988; 1979; 1970; 1961; 1952

Your Six Years Are: 2025; 2016; 2007; 1998; 1989; 1980; 1971; 1962; 1953

Your Seven Years Are: 2026; 2017; 2008; 1999; 1990; 1981; 1972; 1963; 1954

Your Eight Years Are: 2027; 2018; 2009; 2000; 1991; 1982; 1973; 1964; 1955

Your Nine Years Are: 2028; 2019; 2010; 2001; 1992; 1983; 1974; 1965; 1956

If Your First Number Is Four:

Your One Years Are: 2028; 2019; 2010; 2001; 1992; 1983; 1974; 1965; 1956

Your Two Years Are: 2029; 2020; 2011; 2002; 1993; 1984; 1975; 1966; 1957

Your Three Years Are: 2030; 2021; 2012; 2003; 1994; 1985; 1976; 1967; 1958

Your Four Years Are: 2031; 2022; 2013; 2004; 1995; 1986; 1977; 1968; 1959

Your Five Years Are: 2023; 2014; 2005; 1996; 1987; 1978; 1969; 1960; 1951

Your Six Years Are: 2024; 2015; 2006; 1997; 1988; 1979; 1970; 1961; 1952

Your Seven Years Are: 2025; 2016; 2007; 1998; 1989; 1980; 1971; 1962; 1953

Your Eight Years Are: 2026; 2017; 2008; 1999; 1990; 1981; 1972; 1963; 1954

Your Nine Years Are: 2027; 2018; 2009; 2000; 1991; 1982; 1973; 1964; 1955

If Your First Number Is Five:

Your One Years Are: 2027; 2018; 2009; 2000; 1991; 1982; 1973; 1964; 1955

Your Two Years Are: 2028; 2019; 2010; 2001; 1992; 1983; 1974; 1965; 1956

Your Three Years Are: 2029; 2020; 2011; 2002; 1993; 1984; 1975; 1966; 1957

Your Four Years Are: 2030; 2021; 2012; 2003; 1994; 1985; 1976; 1967; 1958

Your Five Years Are: 2031; 2022; 2013; 2004; 1995; 1986; 1977; 1968; 1959

Your Six Years Are: 2023; 2014; 2005; 1996; 1987; 1978; 1969; 1960; 1951

Your Seven Years Are: 2024; 2015; 2006; 1997; 1988; 1979; 1970; 1961; 1952

Your Eight Years Are: 2025; 2016; 2007; 1998; 1989; 1980; 1971; 1962; 1953

Your Nine Years Are: 2026; 2017; 2008; 1999; 1990; 1981; 1972; 1963; 1954

If Your First Number Is Six:

Your One Years Are: 2026; 2017; 2008; 1999; 1990; 1981; 1972; 1963; 1954

Your Two Years Are: 2027; 2018; 2009; 2000; 1991; 1982; 1973; 1964; 1955

Your Three Years Are: 2028; 2019; 2010; 2001; 1992; 1983; 1974; 1965; 1956

Your Four Years Are: 2029; 2020; 2011; 2002; 1993; 1984; 1975; 1966; 1957

Your Five Years Are: 2030; 2021; 2012; 2003; 1994; 1985; 1976; 1967; 1958

Your Six Years Are: 2031; 2022; 2013; 2004; 1995; 1986; 1977; 1968; 1959

Your Seven Years Are: 2023; 2014; 2005; 1996; 1987; 1978; 1969; 1960; 1951

Your Eight Years Are: 2024; 2015; 2006; 1997; 1988; 1979; 1970; 1961; 1952

Your Nine Years Are: 2025; 2016; 2007; 1998; 1989; 1980; 1971; 1962; 1953

If Your First Number Is Seven:

Your One Years Are: 2025; 2016; 2007; 1998; 1989; 1980; 1971; 1962; 1953

Your Two Years Are: 2026; 2017; 2008; 1999; 1990; 1981; 1972; 1963; 1954

Your Three Years Are: 2027; 2018; 2009; 2000; 1991; 1982; 1973; 1964; 1955

Your Four Years Are: 2028; 2019; 2010; 2001; 1992; 1983; 1974; 1965; 1956

Your Five Years Are: 2029; 2020; 2011; 2002; 1993; 1984; 1975; 1966; 1957

Your Six Years Are: 2030; 2021; 2012; 2003; 1994; 1985; 1976; 1967; 1958

Your Seven Years Are: 2031; 2022; 2013; 2004; 1995; 1986; 1977; 1968; 1959

Your Eight Years Are: 2023; 2014; 2005; 1996; 1987; 1978; 1969; 1960; 1951

Your Nine Years Are: 2024; 2015; 2006; 1997; 1988; 1979; 1970; 1961; 1952

If Your First Number Is Eight:

Your One Years Are: 2024; 2015; 2006; 1997; 1988; 1979; 1970; 1961; 1952

Your Two Years Are: 2025; 2016; 2007; 1998; 1989; 1980; 1971; 1962; 1953

Your Three Years Are: 2026; 2017; 2008; 1999; 1990; 1981; 1972; 1963; 1954

Your Four Years Are: 2027; 2018; 2009; 2000; 1991; 1982; 1973; 1964; 1955

Your Five Years Are: 2028; 2019; 2010; 2001; 1992; 1983; 1974; 1965; 1956

Your Six Years Are: 2029; 2020; 2011; 2002; 1993; 1984; 1975; 1966; 1957

Your Seven Years Are: 2030; 2021; 2012; 2003; 1994; 1985; 1976; 1967; 1958

Your Eight Years Are: 2031; 2022; 2013; 2004; 1995; 1986; 1977; 1968; 1959

Your Nine Years Are: 2023; 2014; 2005; 1996; 1987; 1978; 1969; 1960; 1951

If Your First Number Is Nine:

Your One Years Are: 2023; 2014; 2005; 1996; 1987; 1978; 1969; 1960; 1951

Your Two Years Are: 2024; 2015; 2006; 1997; 1988; 1979; 1970; 1961; 1952

Your Three Years Are: 2025; 2016; 2007; 1998; 1989; 1980; 1971; 1962; 1953

Your Four Years Are: 2026; 2017; 2008; 1999; 1990; 1981; 1972; 1963; 1954

Your Five Years Are: 2027; 2018; 2009; 2000; 1991; 1982; 1973; 1964; 1955

Your Six Years Are: 2028; 2019; 2010; 2001; 1992; 1983; 1974; 1965; 1956

Your Seven Years Are: 2029; 2020; 2011; 2002; 1993; 1984; 1975; 1966; 1957

Your Eight Years Are: 2030; 2021; 2012; 2003; 1994; 1985; 1976; 1967; 1958

Your Nine Years Are: 2031; 2022; 2013; 2004; 1995; 1986; 1977; 1968; 1959

Remember my amazed discovery that these ancient principles completely validate Louise Hay's work with affirmations? Her work can also be used to support you in moving through each year, riding the waves instead of fighting the current. The next chapter will give you the affirmations you need for every year in the cycle.

CHAPTER 12

Louise Hay's Affirmations for Each Stage of Your Journey

Just as Louise Hay's affirmations can help you love and accept yourself, they can also be used to help you align with the flow of each year of your life. The phrases below are designed to help support your process as you go through each of the nine years in the cycle. Find the year that you're currently in by using the chart in Chapter 11; then locate the list of affirmations for that year below. Choose at least one, two, or three of those affirmations to work with each day, selecting the ones that appeal to you the most or that catch your eye. But feel free to change it up and use other affirmations within that category, depending on what you sense you need at the time.

One Year

I have the inner resources to figure things out.

I take time to treasure the mysterious and invisible process of life that I am.

I work on healing those areas of my life that need work, and I am patient with the process.

I know I am safe and everything will be all right.

As I quiet down this year, I open myself up to my own healing powers.

My body uses relaxation as a time to repair and rejuvenate itself.

The more I relax, the healthier I am.

I shift my focus from scary thoughts to peaceful thoughts.

I take time to replenish my energy.

Today I leave my past behind. I trust life and know that I am safe.

Inside of me lie all the answers to all the questions I shall ever ask.

I express myself through creative endeavors of all kinds.

I am stronger than I realize.

Life always reveals what I need to know, when I need to know it.

There is a time for birth and a time for death. It is only change.
  I know that life is eternal.

I take time during the day to meditate, daydream, and quiet my mind.
  I feel newly energized after these periods of restfulness.

I have faith in the perfect unfolding of my life.

Today I remember that I have all the time in the world to relax
  and be with the process of life.

I always have access to the One Infinite Source.

I am being prepared for a marvelous transformation.

I trust the process of life.

Two Year

I choose to open my arms to all the good that life has in store for me.

I feel comfortable saying no to what others want me to do and yes to
  my own inner knowing.

I give up trying to learn lessons for anyone else. I see everyone as
  whole, complete, and perfect right here and right now.

I can provide everything I need for myself. I am more capable
  than I know.

Better things are coming. I know it, and I feel it. I look forward
  to each day.

The more I help others, the more I prosper and grow. In my world,
  everybody wins.

I project love and peace. I can see how my inner tranquility
  attracts like-minded people.

*I am now attracting whatever help I need to solve problems.
I am safe.*

I trust in Life to take care of everything for me. All is truly well.

*Cherishing myself gives me the extra energy to work through
any problem more quickly. My life is a labor of love.*

*What I give out, I get back tenfold. Therefore, I give out as
much love as I can.*

I am patient, tolerant, and diplomatic. My words are healing.

I now accept and live the abundant life the Universe offers me.

*I am grateful to others for the kindness they show me.
I am filled with love and appreciation.*

*I choose to see myself harvesting a happy, successful life full
of wonderful experiences.*

Whenever I need help, I ask for it.

I am my own best friend. Today I will do something special for myself.

*I respond to life in a powerful, positive manner. I am not a
victim in any sense of the word.*

*I am open and receptive to all the good in the Universe.
There is nothing that is beyond my grasp.*

*The garden of my life is taking shape. The seeds I have planted are
growing roots beneath the ground and are preparing to burst forth.*

Three Year

I welcome change. It is full of special opportunities.

*I am filled with boundless energy. I awaken each morning eager
for the new experiences to come.*

I can handle any experience or situation that is put in my path.

*I know that many of the questions I have about life can be answered
as I sleep. I clearly remember my dreams when I wake up
each morning.*

*I am so pleased with where I am, and I eagerly look forward
to the future.*

I say it like it is. I feel free to express my opinion.

I am excited to do something different today. I am willing to move out of my comfort zone and experience life in a new way.

I now channel anger as a means to create positive change.

The turning point in my life has come. I am open and receptive to having a future I love.

For every problem that I may create, there is a solution.

I am organized and productive. I have lots of energy, and I enjoy getting my life in order.

I allow myself to succeed. I am far more than my past limited thinking.

I view all experiences as opportunities to learn and grow.

My world is changing for the better.

My inner vision is clear and unclouded.

Forgiveness is a gift to myself that allows me to live freely in the present.

I release the need to blame anyone—including myself.

I am a natural winner in every aspect of my life. I can do whatever I set my mind to, and I choose to only listen to people who support me.

I constantly have new insights and new ways of looking at the world.

I am filled with energy and optimism. I allow the Universe to help me as I progress.

Four Year

I easily adapt to new changes.

I allow divine right action to guide me every moment of the day.

My life grows by leaps and bounds, and I am grateful!

I give a portion of my time to helping others. It is good for my own health.

I am a decisive and productive person. I follow through with tasks that I start.

It is okay to make mistakes while learning. I release myself from the burden of being perfect.

I move forward with confidence and ease.

Every opportunity is valuable to me. I am willing to learn.

Rather than fix problems, I fix my thinking. Then problems fix themselves.

I am guided throughout this day to make all the right choices.

Everything is all right. It is only change. I am safe.

There is no such thing as a bad decision. Every choice I make helps me progress on life's path.

I easily flow with new experiences, new directions, and new changes.

I trust in my power to think. I am clearheaded and open-minded.

I observe myself without judgment or criticism. I am open to possible change.

Every decision that I make is the right decision for me at this time in my life. I am secure and powerful.

I make sure that all my choices support the new pathways I want to take.

I am always at the right place at the right time, doing just the right thing; there is no "wrong" in my life.

I spend time with the elders in my life. I know that they are a source of knowledge and experience and that they have a lot to contribute to my time on Earth.

I choose to be flexible in all areas. I am able to change my point of view as I absorb new thoughts and ideas.

Five Year

I nourish myself by saying no when I mean no, and yes when I mean yes. I know what I want.

All of my family members live harmonious lives.

I act with honor and integrity in all that I do.

I go to sleep each night feeling great contentment. I am at peace.

It is time for me to let go of my old beliefs about how relationships are supposed to be.

In this moment, all is well. There is nowhere I have to go and nothing I have to do.

I enjoy offering encouragement and compliments to others.

I work for the enjoyment and satisfaction—not just to earn a living.

I release the need to criticize. I am unconditionally loving and accepting.

I give to others all the things I wish to receive.

I am calm and centered in times of crisis. I am a comfort to those around me, as well as myself.

All of my friends understand my needs. I have many friends who love me.

I cannot change other people. I accept them the way they are.

Life created me to be fulfilled. I release all expectations and trust in the goodness of the Universe.

I love others and know that they are doing the best they can.

My family gives me loving support every step of the way. I know that I can always count on them and they can always count on me.

I am connected at all times to Universal intelligence. I am happy, whole, and complete.

I appreciate the gifts that the Universe has given me, and I give thanks every day. I am happy to be me.

I forgive my parents for any hurt they may have inflicted on me. I know that they were just doing the best they could with what they knew at the time. I send them love.

I radiate warmth and love. People enjoy being in my presence, and they seek my company. I love the sense of community that I have built around me.

Six Year

I am grateful for all that I have received in life. I deserve the best, and I accept the best now.

I have plenty of time for each task I need to perform today. I am a powerful person because I choose to live in the present moment.

I am perfect just as I am.

At this very moment, enormous wealth and power are available to me.

Gratitude and thanksgiving are a way of life for me. It is as easy as breathing.

I am neither too little nor too much, and I do not have to prove myself to anyone. I am okay just as I am.

I give myself permission to be prosperous.

I take a deep breath and allow myself to relax. My whole body calms down.

This is the moment I take my power back.

I look upon my past, present, and future with love.

I do a mental housecleaning today and make room for an abundance of positive thoughts.

I breathe life into my vision and create the world I deserve.

I am always on time, which is a way of showing respect to myself and those in my life.

I know how to do the work I love, and I am paid well for it.

There is time and space for everything I want to do today.

I choose to feel worthy and deserving.

I am grateful for everything and everyone in my life.

I regularly praise those who work for me or with me. They deserve recognition for the wonderful jobs they do.

I become more proficient every day. There are no limits to my abilities.

I release everything from the past that no longer serves me. I have no regret since I know that all that I have done up till now has led me to the present moment.

Seven Year

I gladly give away that which I no longer need in preparation for getting all that I want.

The world is a work of art and so am I.

I bless with love all of the money that passes through my hands.

No matter what my age, now is the time to live it up, to acknowledge my self-worth.

I follow my higher instincts and listen to my heart in all that I do.

I relax today, only doing those activities that bring me pleasure.

I spend money wisely. I always have as much as I need.

I take the time to savor the beauty of my surroundings. I live in a bountiful, vibrant world.

I am dancing on air because Life loves me.

My thoughts are my best friends. My inner dialogue is kind and loving.

As I quiet down and focus on the beautiful things in my life, I open myself up to my own healing powers.

I am willing to release all patterns of criticism.

My work space is a sacred haven. I treat it with respect and love.

I release the need for lack. I can afford anything that I believe I deserve.

I know that I am doing the best that I can at this moment, so I stop all self-criticism. I love and take care of myself at all times.

There is plenty for everyone on this Earth, including me.

I feel safe in the rhythm and flow of ever-changing life. I am relaxed and alert and experience this day with total pleasure.

I give myself permission to prosper. My consciousness accepts wealth as natural, and I view money as my friend.

I am open and receptive to prosperity in life. My income is never "fixed." It grows as I grow.

I appreciate all of the miracles around me—the setting sun, the ebbing tides, the majesty of mighty mountains—and each day that I live and breathe in this spectacular world. I am grateful for everything.

Eight Year

I am a divine conduit for transforming the quality of other people's lives.

I release the need to struggle. I trust the Universe to take care of me.

My alone time is just as fulfilling as the time I spend with others.

Today I create new memories, filled with peace, goodwill, and compassion for others.

Knowledge is power, and I have unlimited wisdom.

I know how to take care of myself. I am healthier than I have ever been.

I always have the perfect relationships—both at home and at work.

I am patient and at peace with the process of life.

I am grateful for life's generosity. I am blessed.

When I need help, I easily ask for it. I know that the help I need will always arrive at just the right time and in just the right way.

I recognize my body as a good friend.

No matter where I live, I am always safe and secure. I feel at home in any living situation.

I handle all my responsibilities with delight and ease.

I want love and acceptance from my family, so I get the ball rolling by loving and accepting them exactly as they are now.

My home is a warm, peaceful, beautiful haven. Love fills every room.

I treat each person I encounter during the day with kindness. I receive the same consideration in return.

My job is a constant source of joy for me; and I am surrounded by happy, fulfilled people in my work environment.

I am fortunate to be surrounded by neighbors who are friendly, peaceful, dependable, and fun. I value them, and they value me.

I release all self-doubt. I go beyond any feelings of not being capable and creative enough.

My free time is precious to me. I use it wisely and try to spend as much time having fun as I can. I know that my work is only one aspect of my life.

Nine Year

The door of my heart is wide open, and I am safe.

I am in love with every "now" moment. I choose to have fun doing this. I choose to be free.

My life is a party to be shared with everyone I know.

I maintain boundaries yet still remain open to the goodness of others.

I release all the junk from the past. I live in the present moment.

It is healing to show my emotions. It is safe for me to be vulnerable.

I think big every day, and then I allow myself to accept even more.

Joyous ideas are circulating freely within me.

I now attract new friends who are exciting, loving, caring, accepting, funny, and generous.

I allow the playful child within me to emerge and have fun.

I am generous with praise and compliments. I enjoy making other people happy.

This is a new moment. I bless it with love and let it teach me new lessons.

I know that I may have to release some people who are not supportive of me, but I wish them well as they proceed down their paths.

Every day is an adventure. I look forward to the magnificent experiences that this day has to offer.

I love my own company. I am never lonely when I am alone. It is great to be me!

I am a magnet for miracles. My special energy attracts wonderful people and experiences to me.

I express my creativity openly and freely. Laughing, smiling, and dancing are all wonderful parts of my life.

My heart has an endless capacity to love more and more.

My mind is a powerful tool that I can use however I wish. I choose only what is best for me.

My life is filled with love and joy because my life is a divine idea in expression.

These affirmations add to all the knowledge and tools you've gained in the first two parts of this book, from discovering each aspect of your own hidden symmetry to understanding the cycles you pass through as you grow and evolve. In the final chapters, we'll look at how this all comes together, first through Louise's personal experience and then in your own journey.

PART III

WUWEI— ACTION WITHOUT EFFORT

"When the stories of our life no longer bind us, we discover within them something greater. We discover that within the very limitations of form, of our maleness and femaleness, of our parenthood and our childhood, of gravity on the earth and the changing of the seasons, is the freedom and harmony we have sought for so long. Our individual life is an expression of the whole mystery, and in it we can rest in the center of the movement, the center of all worlds."

— JACK KORNFIELD

CHAPTER 13

LOUISE HAY'S HIDDEN SYMMETRY

I first met Louise Hay when she came to one of my workshops. A few weeks before, the organizer had called me to say, "You'll never guess who's coming to your workshop! Louise Hay!"

"Uh, gosh, that's—*fantastic!*" I said, as my knees started knocking together. Since then, I've learned from Louise that this is a common experience. Everyone is so nervous at first to meet the great Louise Hay!

My jitters continued until a moment in the workshop that I still remember so clearly. At the first morning break, Louise threw her arms around me and said, "This is one of the very best workshops I've ever been to!"

Wow, a combination of relief, joy, and pure honor surged through me at that point. Louise participated in the class with great gusto, and since that time has attended many of my workshops and retreats, always the brightest light in the room.

I had to laugh out loud when I discovered Louise's Nine Star Ki numbers: 2.4.3. She and I are both Twos. No wonder I felt an immediate resonance with her on first sight, despite my knocking knees! But that wasn't the only thing that tickled me. Of course a Two would name her company Hay *House*. With the theme of home so closely associated with the Two nature, how perfect to give your business that name rather than Hay, Inc.; Hay Books; or Hay Publishing! Louise said she'd always thought that if she ever started a business, she wanted to name it Hay House—that it just felt right.

Two is the number that most strongly represents the power of the feminine overall, and this is why Louise's focus would naturally be on empowering women. She says, "While everything I teach always applies equally to men and women, my biggest desire has been to empower women. Women have been downtrodden for far too long all over the world, *and* the women raise the male children. Enlightened women can teach little boys how to participate in a joyous, loving, kind world that everyone will want to live in."

The Two also represents holding a place of love for the world as Mother—the Divine Feminine strength, which is total acceptance of who another person is as perfect and lovable. I can easily visualize Louise's powerful affirmations being like the ideal mother's voice in your ear, speaking positive and loving truths for you and your life.

Over the years, I've done readings for many members of the Hay House family. With great delight, I discovered that all of the people I happen to have read have the first numbers of Two, Five, or Eight—personalities based on the themes of home, community, nurturing, and compassionately helping others! Of course, no one was hired because of their birth timing. Instead, this simply shows that a system that's healthy and in balance will attract people who are naturally aligned with its purpose.

In her own journey, Louise is a shining example of what can happen for a Two at midlife when that door opens to offer a way to step into their power. It wasn't until her 50s that she really became the figure we now know, and she founded Hay House as she entered her 60s. Not every Two will be able to go through that door when it opens, though. The less conscious they are and the less personal work they've done, the less likely it is that they'll even notice the opportunity, let alone take advantage of it. I believe that the degree of personal power a Two can attain in the second half of life depends on the amount of inner work they've done in the first half, as well as the continuing effort they make from there. Louise's achievements are certainly a testament to her personal work all these years, which I see her still devoted to every day.

So we certainly see Louise's Two nature showing up in her life, but most people haven't been privy to her emotional self, her Four. This second number shows her inner adaptability but also potential feelings of uncertainty in times of stress. This can also result in a kind of *Get me out of here!* reaction that makes someone want to flee—at the worst, a desire to get out of *life*. Louise shared with me that because of the terrible abuse and trauma she suffered as a young child, when she was nine years old, she ate what she thought were poison berries in an attempt to escape. She lay down to die, only to discover that the berries her mother had always warned her about weren't deadly after all. It hurts my heart to even begin to imagine what that little girl went through.

And then we turn to Louise's third number: Three. This is the most entrepreneurial of all the numbers, so it's no surprise that she started the business of Hay House and was able to make it such a great success. And even in the specifics of her work with affirmations, recall that one fundamental theme of Three has to do with what you say to yourself, and another theme is about change. So how perfect it is that Louise's destiny might have to do with changing your thoughts!

Hope, optimism, growth, and change are all patterns that run deep in the Three Warrior purpose as a catalyst, an agent of positive change for the world. Certainly we can see Louise fully living her true calling here, and millions around the world have benefited in the process.

Mileposts

In our conversations for this book, Louise and I sat down to talk about time—the different phases of her life and what each year and decade brought. It was fascinating to see how the mileposts of her life fit into the themes of the years. The major turning point for her work was 1988, the year she appeared on both Oprah Winfrey's and Phil Donahue's talk shows within the same week.

(Interestingly, both Oprah and Phil are also Twos!) That was a Four year for Louise, a time when a person of influence is likely to show up to open doors in some way. Louise attributes her interview with Oprah as being the point in her career where things just exploded, as so many more people were introduced to her work.

Interestingly, the next time Louise was on Oprah's show, in 2008, it was no longer a time when she was so focused on trying to reach more people. Instead, she was honored as a woman of power who'd helped so many and accomplished so much. And again the energy of that event aligned with the pattern of the year. Instead of it being a year when someone influential would lend a hand, 2008 was a Six year for Louise, a period that's about getting respect and recognition for all that she'd achieved!

As we talked about the different cycles of time, I wondered if Louise had set an intention for what she wanted to accomplish in each phase of her life. But she said that's not how she lived. There was no intention set for any particular stage, or any goal in mind as she traveled on her remarkable journey.

She explained, "No, it's not about intention. I do what Life presents to me. I've learned to trust what comes to me. If it's a challenging lesson, okay, what do I need to do? If it's a door opening, wonderful! I can do it. Whatever challenge or opportunity is given to me, the wherewithal just unfolds. I allow my life to happen."

Well, be still my heart! This was music to my ears because this is the core principle that Chinese medicine and philosophy teaches about how to live: *action without effort*. Rather than trying to *make* things happen, Louise allowed. She was able to surrender to the process and go with the flow of the time. This is especially impressive when we look at her third number. Anyone with a Three in this position will have a tendency to push—to try to force things or think they have to take charge and figure it all out. Usually the last thing they'd do is let go and trust, but this is exactly what Louise did. Many times I've heard her say this about how her work grew over the years: "I just did what was in front of me."

This way of being is a reflection of the profound inner work Louise has done to always bring greater levels of balance and health to her life, and it's yet another validation of her work by Chinese medicine.

Just as each of her affirmations fits perfectly with these universal principles from ancient times, her personal work in her own life has used the same paradigm to help achieve her greatest potential. Louise became whole by transcending the worry and lack of confidence of the Two nature to claim her compassionate power, the uncertainty and self-doubt of the Four to move forward anyway, and the urgency and drive of the Three to just do what needed to be done—and in the process, change the world!

In the next chapter, I'll share with you some ways you can accomplish the same in your own life, by aligning with your nature and allowing your life to unfold effortlessly.

CHAPTER 14

FIND YOUR WUWEI

In Chinese, there's a term to convey the concept of action without effort: *wuwei* (pronounced "woo-way"). Very simply, here is what it means: A tree doesn't try to grow; it just grows. When you live in accordance with your nature, you don't have to try to reach some goal, to figure out what to do to get what you want. In fact, your goals—those things you *think* you want—are most likely just symptoms of your current imbalance and aren't always to be trusted!

Most of us spend our days lost in our heads, trying to come up with the answer to what to do and when and how to do it, in order to get out of this place we don't want to be so that we can finally find happiness. Yet it's not about figuring out what to *do;* it's about what to *be.*

If we're aligned with nature, we can just be, and our actions effortlessly ride the ebb and flow of life. But we can't do this if we are unable to relax in the truth of who we are. Most of us go through life almost blaming ourselves for our nature, which creates resistance in the system and stops the flow.

We can't actively pursue wuwei. We live with wuwei when we allow our feelings without being swept away by them and our thoughts without believing every one of them. Unfortunately, most of us are caught up in the constant commentary going on in our heads that only keeps us locked into certain belief patterns, and doing rather than being.

Self-Judgment

I recently gave a presentation about Chinese face reading at an exclusive retreat to a standing-room-only group full of highly spiritual women, most of whom had been doing serious personal work for decades. The previous day, many had shared stories about the amazing progress they'd made in their lives after years of work. They'd healed traumas or illnesses or found a way to pursue what they truly loved.

After my talk, however, nearly everyone who stepped up to speak with me said with a fierce charge in her voice, "I *hate* this wrinkle!" or "I can't *stand* my nose!" The energy behind each statement was palpable—I could feel how intense that emotion was and how toxic to the speaker on so many levels. It was hard to believe that these were the same women who'd conquered illness, recovered from abuse, and learned to be powerful healers for others, for they were carrying such a negative charge about some small aspect of their face they judged as bad.

We *all* have a tendency to view ourselves this harshly, seemingly hardwired to look for what's wrong with us and focus on the negative, and this is due to a great extent upon our conditioning from birth. We live in a culture where we're taught to view everything as "either/or": It's either good or bad, right or wrong. We categorize everything this way, and it leads us into the trap of thinking that if only we could get rid of the "bad," then everything would be all right.

If I asked you to make a list of everything wonderful about yourself and then a list of anything about yourself that needs to be changed, I hope that you'd first come up with a list full of things you love. But it's likely that your second list of what's "wrong" with you would be longer, and you'd be cringing and grimacing in self-judgment as you wrote it. And as they viewed their two lists, most people would conclude that if only they could eliminate all of their "bad" qualities, this would leave all the good ones, and they'd finally be happy.

This way of thinking is a part of the reason why the Western mind hasn't been as easily able to understand the interconnectedness of all life as the Eastern mind does. In Asian culture, there's a more holistic or global view of things, rather than judging them as one thing or the other. There have even been scientific studies that show this, finding that when a Westerner looks at a painting, they immediately focus on one individual object in the image— the tree in the foreground or a person standing in the scene. Then they look for another single object and move on from there.

When an Asian person views the same painting, they look at both foreground and background *at the same time*, taking in the whole picture instead of choosing any one detail. So there's no "either/or"; instead, there's a perception of the symmetrical whole. It's a global way of thinking. To understand this, it can help to visualize the Earth: It has a North Pole *and* a South Pole. It can't possibly have a North Pole *or* a South Pole. It always has both.

When it comes to looking at our personal characteristics, using this Asian way of perceiving things can really help us break free of our restrictive Western viewpoint. Instead of thinking we have to eradicate the "bad" parts of ourselves, we see that they're actually one aspect of the whole. We can think of it as everything having a front and a back. If we look on the other side of any weakness we think we have, we discover a corresponding strength. They're interconnected, so if we got rid of the weakness, we'd also lose the strength.

Any one part of your nature that's proving to be a challenge for you needs to be understood within the context of the whole. When you look at something about yourself that you think is negative, can you discover what positive quality might be its partner? If you're a Four, can you see how your indecisiveness has another side that reveals your adaptability and gentle way with people? As a Three, does the frequency of your frustration match your level of drive—how goal oriented and hardworking you are? Could it be possible that there's nothing you need to get rid of at all, but can instead look at bringing the two sides into balance?

Acupuncture for the Spirit

Chinese medicine teaches that your body is very wise; if it's in balance, it can heal itself. The goal of the acupuncturist is not to figure out how to fix whatever's wrong with you but instead to bring your system back into balance so that it will naturally heal itself.

We all have cancer cells in our bodies all the time. So why do some of us get sick and others don't? Chinese medicine believes that if our system is in balance, it eliminates the malignant cells naturally. But if we get too stressed and too far out of balance, the body is not able to clear them effectively.

My work is often called "acupuncture for the spirit" because it applies that understanding to your life on a spirit level. If any part of you is in self-judgment, or if you hold a charge around some aspect of your past, it puts stress in the system and over time will throw it out of balance. This may or may not eventually cause illness in the body, but it can definitely keep you stuck in life, locked into creating your future based on your past. Those toxic thoughts and feelings flood your mind and heart, and in that state, is it possible to be wuwei? No way!

So how can you rebalance? How can you move beyond the self-judgment you hold and all the ways you don't love yourself? One elegantly simple way is to use the powerful affirmations in this book that Louise created for your personal numbers, because their words support you to embrace your unique nature so that you can move toward it in strength and love. Another is to use what you've learned about yourself in this book to come home to yourself, to relax into a new understanding and acceptance of who you really are.

When I teach professional trainings for people to coach and consult using this work, I do in-depth demonstrations of readings for a variety of volunteers while the students observe. A few years ago, one of the subjects was David, a 1.5.1 musician with exotic tattoos and piercings. He was a highly creative but deeply emotional man who was carrying a lot of painful judgment about

himself. He couldn't understand what was the matter with him. Why did he crave so much time alone and feel things so deeply when others let things just roll off their backs?

David's girlfriend complained that he didn't talk to her, but he was overwhelmed when she wanted to download everything that passed through her consciousness onto him. And while he had found success as a musician, it was more important to him to have freedom in how he lived his life and did his work rather than chase money to get a big house and fancy car. Yet now he wondered if he was wrong not to feel driven like his younger brother was.

As I did the reading and explained the One nature to him, David listened intently. When I was done, there was a long silence. He just sat there, looking in my eyes for what felt like forever, and then finally said, "You mean, I'll always be this way?"

I took a breath and had a bit of an *Uh-oh!* moment in my mind. Was he viewing this as a prison he'd never escape? But an instant later, he let out an enormous sigh and flashed a big smile, exclaiming, "That is such a relief! You mean I'm *supposed* to be like this!"

He got it. This was his nature; he was designed to be exactly this way. There was nothing wrong with him—or rather, the only thing wrong with him was that he *thought* there was something wrong! Like all of us, through a lifetime of accumulated negative self-judgment, there was enormous tension in this young man's system that kept him from loving and accepting himself.

David's patterns of thought, emotion, and behavior weren't his fault and they weren't a problem. In fact, it was his resistance to them that was causing the problem. Like all of us, he was born with his inner design shining brightly in full joy, ready to begin the journey. But also like all of us, nearly from the moment he was born, he was receiving messages from the outside world that began to diminish his spirit.

Stepping Out of Your Story

As much as your parents truly love and adore you, they have unconsciously projected certain expectations onto you from the beginning, and they can feel stressed and confused when you don't conform to that image. Add to this your experience with the rest of your family, teachers, peers, and community—as well as what our society defines as acceptable and valued—and you're soon immersed in an environment of subtle and not-so-subtle judgments about who you're supposed to be. To one degree or another, the implicit message that you receive is, *You'll be loved if you're like that, not this.* Well, of course you want to be loved, so you try to be more like *that,* and thus begins the journey away from original nature. By the end of childhood, you have a negative talk-radio station playing in your head, telling you all the ways you're wrong; and because of that, you make choices that lead you to navigate farther and farther off course.

The parts of yourself you judge as wrong are the ones you try to run away from, while you cling to the few parts that you see as right. In fact, that just amplifies the problem. You're a global being with your own North Pole and South Pole—both part of the whole, neither wrong nor right. When you can see the entire picture, you can discover how to navigate your thoughts and feelings in a more successful way.

One of the beautiful gifts of discovering your hidden symmetry is the realization that there's a design to all of your various parts and pieces, that you are part of nature. You were intended to be exactly this, just as the oak tree was designed to grow acorns. The oak tree has no angst about the acorns that sprout among its leaves. It doesn't cringe about the girth of its trunk, and it doesn't strive to be more like the eucalyptus next door. It is fully, vitally, joyfully oak. When you understand that you are one of nature's designs just like every living thing on this planet, and that your patterns have a purpose, it takes you out of your story—that background commentary that's been looping through your mind for decades about what's wrong with you and how you should change.

When Pulitzer Prize–winning poet Philip Schultz was interviewed about his struggle with dyslexia as a child, he talked about how liberating it was to finally discover that it was not his fault, that it was due to an issue in his brain. It was this realization that empowered him to finally be able to learn to read. He said, "When someone gives you the opportunity to step outside of your current reality, it changes the story you've been telling yourself. It can change the entire course of your life."

Everything has a front and a back, a symmetry to it. It may well be that this poet's dyslexia is one side of the same quality that makes him such a creative soul, his nonlinear artistic mind much more likely to have letters and words shimmy in unconventional ways inside his brain. It's fascinating that after he discovered that this wasn't his personal failing, he was finally able to learn to read by imagining himself as a separate little ten-year-old boy who *could* read, and then—he could! He'd been so lost and stressed by his story that it had prevented him from being able to learn. By letting go of that, he was free to become the boy who could read.

Whatever story it is that you're telling yourself, it's made up of an intricate and coherent pattern of repeating thoughts and feelings, many of which you were never taught to recognize and honor but instead to judge and resist. Nine Star Ki reveals the subtle details of your unique journey, but it also gives you an important gift: You were meant to be this way. You will always be this way.

Every thought or feeling that passes through your consciousness is just a tiny reflection of your total inner design, and there's nothing the matter with any of it. You're part of nature and that's never wrong. The only thing that's out of place is how you've been unable to relax and love all of it. When you realize that none of this is something you personally caused or need to fix, when you recognize it as your intended design, then you no longer judge; you just allow and observe.

We don't worry when the sun rises so early in the summer or panic when the leaves fall off the trees in autumn. These are part of the symmetry of nature, and so are all of your qualities as well. Rather than getting swept away by your feelings and then having to find your way back to center, just watch them soar through your consciousness like birds fluttering by, and you'll find you're still standing, grounded and in balance. As you are more and more able to do this, the difficulties you used to struggle with disappear from your life.

Author Steven Hayes, Ph.D., originator of Acceptance and Commitment Therapy (ACT), compares this behavior to the way you might struggle with a toy called a Chinese finger trap. When you put your fingers into it, the woven bamboo tube constricts around them; the more you try to pull to get your fingers out, the more firmly it holds them. The only solution is actually to push them deeper into the tube, which makes it relax its grip. Fighting against who you are keeps you locked in battle, confused and stuck. Only by moving fully into yourself can you find freedom. The work is not to change or fix your thoughts and feelings but to change your relationship to them and how you react.

In *My Stroke of Insight,* neuroscientist Jill Bolte Taylor explains how to accomplish this by sharing the startling discovery that it really only takes *90 seconds* for your system to process an emotion. The moment you have an emotion, chemicals are released by your brain and surge through your body to cause physiological changes. But 90 seconds after that sequence is triggered, the chemicals have completely passed out of your bloodstream.

In other words, if you become angry, your system gets swept away in anger for minute and a half. If you remain angry after that time, it's because consciously or unconsciously, you've chosen to stay there. You are actually completely in charge of whether you click back into the feeling again after that brief time has passed.

The reason an emotion continues after 90 seconds is because we're so used to it that we believe it as reality. We get swept up into the story we know so well about who we are and what our life experience is. Again and again, we re-create that emotion the moment its effects begin to fade from our physical body and in the same way, we re-create our "story," continuing to manifest our future based on our past.

So, just as with the Chinese finger trap, the way to change your relationship with your experience is to relax into it, which will help you let go of how you habitually used to react. Remember that your thoughts and emotions are simply patterns of nature, not something you're doing wrong. Really, all any feeling wants is to be welcomed with tenderness. When you can recognize your emotions, perceptions, and behaviors as being simple expressions of your natural design, it liberates you to step out of your story and love whatever comes.

A Seven's thoughts will always tend toward self-criticism and still move to create beauty in the world; a Nine will always fear rejection, yet radiate affection; a Five will always crave appreciation but selflessly offer support, just as an oak grows acorns and a bird sings its insistent song. A feeling is just a feeling. Let it come and watch it go—another will come right after. These are the beautiful waves of energy implicit in your hidden symmetry. The more you can let yourself surf those waves, the more ease and the less stress you'll have in your system, and life will just unfold. When you're in balance, you're in alignment with nature—wuwei—and like that tree, you just grow.

AFTERWORD

Moving Forward

You can use Nine Star Ki to discover the beautiful symmetry of your own inner plan, as well as the hidden design imprinted in the lives of the people around you. The more you develop your knowledge of the elements and numbers, the more insights you'll gain, the more "Aha!" moments you'll have that can help you create a life that's in alignment with your true nature. This is not about finding out what's "wrong" with you or anyone else. It's about discovering how to harmonize your unique qualities so that you can live in a healthy and positive way.

One of the best ways to develop your skills with Nine Star Ki is through simple observation. Once you know someone's numbers, keep them in mind. As you pay attention, you'll be fascinated by how these characteristics emerge in any interaction you have with them and by what you notice about their strengths, challenges, beliefs, and desires—and the story they're continuing to tell themselves about who they are and what life is like.

You may find that you're amazed by how easily you can see these qualities at play in everyone else's life; yet when it comes to understanding your own three numbers, you might relate strongly to some of the descriptions, but not be able to discern some of your most important patterns. This is because you're too close. None of us can fully see our own "stuff," so it can be fun to use this book with friends, to let them read the descriptions of your numbers and point out how they're apparent in ways you never recognized!

And I really should warn you, this can be addicting! When you meet someone new, you may immediately try to find some excuse to ask their birth date; when someone's in the public eye,

you'll be jumping online to research when they were born. One easy way to keep up with things is to check my website, where you'll find free tips and stories and where you can ask questions or share comments: **www.jeanhaner.com**.

If I were to do a personal reading for you, I'd look at the design in both your birth date and the features of your face, because the messages communicated in your face can modify the imprint of your birth date, and reveal other important aspects of who you came here to be. Together, these present the most complete picture of your true inner spirit, far more than any other system I've ever found. If you're looking for the next step, I'd recommend learning about Chinese face reading in order to see how other qualities of your personality and life map are revealed in your face. (You can find lots of free information about face reading on my website as well.)

You were born with a unique spirit that is yours and yours alone, yet which is also a part of the greater patterns of the whole of nature. The more fully you can embrace yourself for who you really are, the more you can move into a place of confidence and compassion, where you can fulfill your sacred purpose in the world. I'll meet you there.

ACKNOWLEDGMENTS

I'm over-the-moon grateful to my soul sister Louise Hay for her loving recognition and support of my work. In the process of writing this book, we discovered that our ancestors emigrated from the same part of what is now the Czech Republic to Chicago at about the same time, so who knows—perhaps our essence is literally intertwined in past generations! What I do know for sure is that we share the same spirit ancestors, guiding us to share messages of love in the world, and I'm dumbstruck with honor and awe that I get to do so in such great company.

I also want to thank Laurel Kelly and John Sims for their boundless love and generosity to me on so many levels, and for giving me unlimited petting access to their cat, Junior, every time I'm in town. (Thank you, too, Junior.) How did I get so lucky? Thanks to my sister and brother-in-law, Diane and Eric Anderson, for all their love over the years; and to Jeffrey Wai-Ming Dong for his influence on this material and for being a man I'm so proud to call my son.

Deep bow to all my teachers, including Lorie Dechar, Jon Sandifer, and William Spear; as well as a big thanks to my absolute queen of an editor, Shannon Littrell, and to friends Beth Atchison and Ruth Mikos for their patient research of birth dates!

Thank you also to everyone who has worked with me in exploring the miracles of their hidden symmetry over the years and to those of you still to come. You'll never know how deeply you touch my heart.

ABOUT THE AUTHOR

 **Jean Haner**, a 2.7.9 and the author of *The Wisdom of Your Face* and *The Wisdom of Your Child's Face*, teaches compassionate and affirming ways for you to understand your true nature and to feel love for everyone in your life, including that reflection in the mirror. With her 30-year background in ancient Chinese principles of balance and health, Jean is well known for providing fascinating and practical information that can be put to immediate use in your life.

Jean married into a Chinese family when she was in her 20s and first began to learn about Chinese culture, philosophy, and medicine from her very traditional mother-in-law. It wasn't until after her wedding that she discovered the family had had her birth date evaluated to see if she was a 'lucky' match for her husband, and that even the date and time of the ceremony had been determined according to what would bring the most luck for the family.

She went on to study the deeper foundations of what the ancient Chinese had discovered about the cycles of time with many teachers over the years, and learned that it has nothing to do with luck and everything to do with learning to be true to your nature.

For free updates and information on Jean's readings, workshops and professional trainings, visit her website.

www.jeanhaner.com

Hay House Titles of Related Interest

YOU CAN HEAL YOUR LIFE, the movie, starring Louise L. Hay & Friends
(available as a 1-DVD programme and an expanded 2-DVD set)
Watch the trailer at: **www.LouiseHayMovie.com**

THE SHIFT, the movie,
starring Dr Wayne W. Dyer
(available as a 1-DVD programme and an expanded 2-DVD set)
Watch the trailer at: **www.DyerMovie.com**

◠

ALL IS WELL: Heal Your Body with Medicine, Affirmations, and Intuition,
by Louise L. Hay and Mona Lisa Schulz, MD, PhD

ARCHETYPES: Who Are You? by Caroline Myss

*THE ART OF EXTREME SELF-CARE: Transform Your Life One Month
at a Time,* by Cheryl Richardson

*DEEP TRUTH: Igniting the Memory of Our Origin, History, Destiny,
and Fate,* by Gregg Braden

*DYING TO BE ME: My Journey from Cancer, to Near Death,
to True Healing,* by Anita Moorjani

All of the above are available at your local bookstore,
or may be ordered by contacting Hay House (see next page).

◠

We hope you enjoyed this Hay House book. If you'd like to receive our online catalog featuring additional information on Hay House books and products, or if you'd like to find out more about the Hay Foundation, please contact:

Hay House UK, Ltd.,
Astley House, 33 Notting Hill Gate, London W11 3JQ
Phone: 0-20-3675-2450 • *Fax:* 0-20-3675-2451
www.hayfoundation.org • **www.hayhouse.co.uk**

✐

Published and distributed in the United States by:
Hay House, Inc., P.O. Box 5100, Carlsbad, CA 92018-5100 • *Phone:* (760) 431-7695
or (800) 654-5126 • *Fax:* (760) 431-6948 or (800) 650-5115
www.hayhouse.com®

Published and distributed in Australia by: Hay House Australia Pty. Ltd.,
18/36 Ralph St., Alexandria NSW 2015 • *Phone:* 612-9669-4299
Fax: 612-9669-4144 • www.hayhouse.com.au

Published and distributed in the Republic of South Africa by: Hay House SA
(Pty), Ltd., P.O. Box 990, Witkoppen 2068 • *Phone/Fax:* 27-11-467-8904
www.hayhouse.co.za

Published in India by: Hay House Publishers India, Muskaan Complex,
Plot No. 3, B-2, Vasant Kunj, New Delhi 110 070 • *Phone:* 91-11-4176-1620
Fax: 91-11-4176-1630 • www.hayhouse.co.in

Distributed in Canada by: Raincoast, 9050 Shaughnessy St., Vancouver, B.C.
V6P 6E5 *Phone:* (604) 323-7100 • *Fax:* (604) 323-2600 • www.raincoast.com

✐

Take Your Soul on a Vacation

Visit **www.HealYourLife.com®** to regroup, recharge,
and reconnect with your own magnificence.
Featuring blogs, mind-body-spirit news, and
life-changing wisdom from Louise Hay and friends.

Visit **www.HealYourLife.com** today!

JOIN THE HAY HOUSE FAMILY

As the leading self-help, mind, body and spirit publisher in the UK, we'd like to welcome you to our family so that you can enjoy all the benefits our website has to offer.

 EXTRACTS from a selection of your favourite author titles

 **COMPETITIONS, PRIZES & SPECIAL OFFERS** Win extracts, money off, downloads and so much more

 **LISTEN** to a range of radio interviews and our latest audio publications

 **CELEBRATE YOUR BIRTHDAY** An inspiring gift will be sent your way

 **LATEST NEWS** Keep up with the latest news from and about our authors

 **ATTEND OUR AUTHOR EVENTS** Be the first to hear about our author events

 **iPHONE APPS** Download your favourite app for your iPhone

 **HAY HOUSE INFORMATION** Ask us anything, all enquiries answered

join us online at **www.hayhouse.co.uk**

 Astley House, 33 Notting Hill Gate
London W11 3JQ
T: 020 3675 2450 E: info@hayhouse.co.uk